Street Smarts from Christian Martial Arts

40 LIFE LESSONS FROM A KARATE MASTER

J. BROWN

Street Smarts from Christian Martial Arts

Edited by Wendy Williamson

Cover design by Wendy Williamson

Agapy Publishing
Charleston, IL
Website: http://www.agapy.com
Email: custserv@agapy.com

International Standard Book Number–13: 978-0-9721328-5-5

International Standard Book Number–10: 0-9721328-5-6

Library of Congress Catalog Card Number: 2006931998

First Edition, 2006

Printed in the United States of America

Table of Contents

Acknowledgements

First, I would like to acknowledge my Lord and Savior, Jesus Christ; it is only because of Him that I was able to write this book. I am grateful that God has given me an abundance of blessings in life and the ability to share many of them with you. Second, I would like to recognize all of the people in my life that God worked through in order to help me bring this book to fruition. These people include my family members, who have been extremely supportive over the years, martial artists from whom I've had the privilege of learning, and finally my brothers and sisters from church and school who have played a significant role in enriching my spiritual life.

Symbol of this Book

A **symbol** is the representation of an idea or concept. All ideas and concepts are symbolic and communicate things that we cannot speak through words. I chose to represent my book with a symbol because it holds something deeper than I can speak or write to you in the following chapters. If you don't remember anything else in this book, it is my hope that the symbol will resonate in your mind. For Christianity is rich with symbols that hold deep spiritual meaning and speak to the heart and soul.

Therefore, allow me a moment to put this symbol into perspective. It partially represents the Trinity. God is one and complete (whole), yet at the same time, He exists as three persons. In the symbol, the three sides of the outer triangle represent the Father, Son, and Holy Spirit. The three sides of the middle triangle represent human life (mind, body, spirit). The two triangles together represent how the Father, Son, and Holy Spirit hold (or contain) complete human life and all that is within.

You probably noticed that the outer triangle holds the middle triangle, but is not connected to it. While we exist within the realm of God, we are not naturally connected to Him because of our sin. Our sin separates us from God and the only way we can become reunited with Him is through Christ. This brings me to the center of the symbol; in the third triangle, you will notice a cross. The cross encapsulates the theme that I hope you pick up in this book...that our lives are connected to God through Christ.

The positioning of the cross also has meaning. It is in the center of the symbol because it represents our Christian faith as the hope for our salvation and highest priority. It is located at the heart of the heavenly and the human domain. It reminds us of our eternal salvation through Jesus Christ's death on the cross and the strength inside each one of us that radiates from the cross. Both pictorially and metaphorically, everything centers on the cross. It is in and through Christ that we live.

Preface

As a Christian martial arts master, I am eager to share some important lessons for training your life. For a long time I mistakenly thought, as so many others do, that the martial arts were only about physical training. It wasn't until after I had earned my first black belt that I realized that the mental and spiritual aspects were actually more important than the physical. My hope is that this book points the way for you and other people who may not be so bent on learning life's lessons by trial and error.

When I was young, I made the mistake of separating and compartmentalizing the different aspects of my life. I used to think that what I learned in the *dojo*[1] stayed in the dojo. When I passed through the double doors of the dojo, I would leave behind the respect, humility, discipline, and self-control that I practiced in karate class. It was almost as if I was living two separate lives. During class, I was one person and when I left and entered the world that contained my home, school, work, and social life, I was someone else.

For the longest time I could not figure out why my instructor insisted that we refer to him by his title outside of class as well as inside of class. I later came to realize that the doors of the dojo did not affect him. He was the same person in all aspects of his life, regardless of where he was or what he was doing. I wanted this transparency in my life, too. I wanted to be <u>one</u> complete human being. Moreover, I wanted the street smarts to become the person and fulfill the purpose that God had planned for me.

Being a Christian martial artist can equip you with all the street smarts you'll need to be one person with purpose. Like the 40 days that Jesus spent preparing for His ministry, may these 40 life lessons help prepare you for your life.

---

[1] A Japanese term referring to a martial arts training center.

Introduction

Life Lesson: You are not merely a body, mind, and spirit... you are the balance you have in each and between the three.

BODY

When speaking of the body, this book refers to the physical or material portion of a human being. The Bible offers further explanation. In 1 Corinthians 3:16[2], we learn that our bodies are the temple of God, and 1 Corinthians 6:20[3] tells us that we are the most valuable life on Earth. Our value is so great that Jesus died a horrible death in order to redeem us and ensure our salvation. Therefore, it is our duty to take care of our bodies so that we can honor God with them. Ephesians 5:29[4] states that nobody ever hates his own body, but always takes steps to sustain it.

The best way we can take care of our bodies is to eat healthy and exercise regularly, and of course stop harmful substances from entering it. Does this mean limiting our diet to only vegetables and exercising three or more hours a day? No, because moderation and balance is important. In addition, the quantity and type of food we consume, as well as the amount of exercise we need, varies drastically from person to person. Popeye needed a different diet and exercise routine than Olive Oil, didn't he? As in all things, moderation and balance must be taken in context with one's individual needs.

---

[2] 1 Corinthians 3:16 – Don't you know that you yourselves are God's temple and that God's Spirit lives in you?

[3] 1 Corinthians 6:20 – You were bought at a price. Therefore honor God with your body.

[4] Ephesians 5:29 – After all, no one ever hated his own body, but he feeds and cares for it, just as Christ does the church.

In addition to moderation and balance, variation is also important. There is a big push these days (and rightfully so) to eat a wide variety of foods and to cross-train. Cross training is engaging in multiple kinds of exercises instead of just engaging in one single activity repeatedly. For example, someone might ride a bike one day, jog the next, and swim another. We see this happening more and more in today's athletes. I know of a football coach who had his players do aerobics as one way to balance bulky muscle and keep agile for games.

There are three good reasons for cross training. First, a wide variety of activities will keep your workouts exciting. Second, your body needs to rest and recover from working the same muscle group over and over again. If you alternate your workouts, you can concentrate on one aspect of exercise while your body is simultaneously healing from another. The third and most important reason for cross training is the need for physical balance. Flexibility, cardiovascular endurance, and muscular strength are all essential for ultimate fitness, and will only enhance different types of physical activity.

Because our bodies are so complex, the best way we can care for them is with moderation, balance, and variation both in what goes in and what comes out (that is, in the form of energy), based on what we know and understand to be natural, healthy, and beneficial. If we keep from being extreme, imbalanced, and stagnant in our lives, then our bodies should be healthy and function correctly. In this way, we can honor God with our bodies and do all that He asks us to do on Earth.

MIND

When speaking of the mind, this book refers to the part of a person that thinks, feels, wishes and chooses. The Bible further explains what the mind is and how it should be used. Job 28:15-18[5] defines wisdom as being an extremely valuable ability of the mind, so much so that it cannot be purchased with even the finest material commodities. The same set of verses tells us that even our finest jewels do not compare with the value of wisdom. So how do we get this awesome ability? After all, it doesn't just grow on trees.

Following God and leaning on Him is the best way to gain wisdom. James 1:5 tells us to ask God for wisdom and it shall be given to us. Solomon asked for wisdom in 1 Kings 3:9[6], and he became one of the wisest men that ever lived. Proverbs 3:13[7] promises that those who seek wisdom will be blessed and receive a lucrative return on their investment. Proverbs 4:6-7[8] reminds us that the effort we put into gaining wisdom is for our benefit because we will be protected and watched over.

---

[5] Job 28:15-18 – It cannot be bought with the finest gold, nor can its price be weighed in silver. It cannot be bought with the gold of Ophir, with precious onyx or sapphires. Neither gold nor crystal can compare with it, nor can it be had for jewels of gold. Coral and jasper are not worthy of mention; the price of wisdom is beyond rubies.

[6] 1 Kings 3:9 – Give your servant a discerning heart to govern your people and to distinguish between right and wrong.

[7] Proverbs 3:13 – Blessed is the man who finds wisdom, the man who gains understanding.

[8] Proverbs 4:6-7 – Do not forsake wisdom, and she will protect you; love her, and she will watch over you. Wisdom is supreme; therefore get wisdom. Though it cost all you have, get understanding.

Despite the fact that wisdom is so important, we are cautioned in 1 Corinthians 1:25[9] not to be too wrapped up in the pursuit of our own wisdom (the wisdom of Man). We can become sidetracked, misled, and unbalanced when we rely too much on the wisdom of Man and not enough on the wisdom of God. So, what is the difference? The Bible tells us in Isaiah 55:8-9 that God's wisdom results in a prosperous eternity and Man's wisdom results in a material, temporary prosperity. Both are important, but one is obviously more valuable than the other is when looking at ourselves from an eternal perspective.

From a mortal perspective, we must also strive for a healthy balance of the mind. Too much of any one thing is bad for the mind, whether it be work or play. Certainly, we should continue to exercise our mind by challenging it with new and different things; however, like our physical self, our mental self needs moderation and variation, too. Moreover, our mental self needs to relax. It's good to engage your mind in a variety of activities in order to keep your interest, prevent fatigue, and maintain an overall positive mental health. It's also good to take time out to rest and sleep, so that God can speak to you and recharge your batteries so to speak.

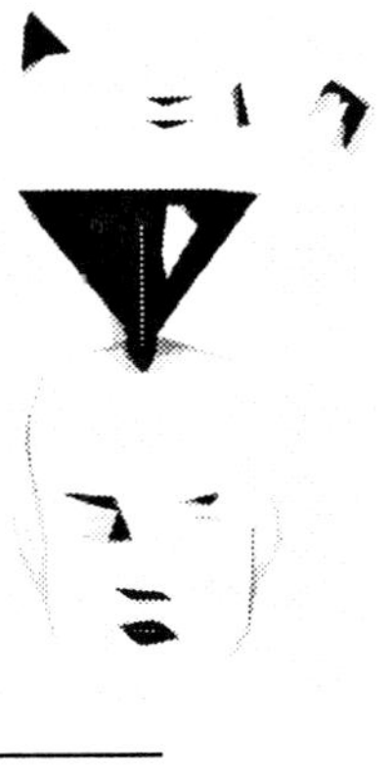

[9] 1 Corinthians 1:25 – For the foolishness of God is wiser than man's wisdom, and the weakness of God is stronger than man's strength.

SPIRIT

When speaking of the spirit, this book refers partly to that which contains a person's moral nature. However, it also refers to religious life. The Bible further explains what the spirit is and how it should be used in Deuteronomy 8:3[10], Proverbs 18:14[11], Romans 8:5-6[12], and Galatians 5:22-23[13].

- Deuteronomy 8:3 reveals that our physical side does not complete what it means to be human, and thus implies the existence of more.
- Proverbs 18:14 indicates that our spirit sustains us through difficult times. This verse also tells us that a healthy and mature spiritual life will help us through all types of trials and tribulations.
- Romans 8:5-6 shows us that there is death for sinful people, but life and peace for those whose mind is controlled by the Spirit. If we let go and allow our minds to be controlled by the Spirit, then we will experience true living and harmony.

---

[10] Deuteronomy 8:3 b – Man does not live on bread alone but on every word that comes from the mouth of the Lord.

[11] Proverbs 18:14 – A man's spirit sustains him in sickness, but a crushed spirit who can bear?

[12] Romans 8:5-6 – Those who live according to the sinful nature have their minds set on what that nature desires; but those who live in accordance with the Spirit have their minds set on what the Spirit desires. The mind of sinful man is death, but the mind controlled by the Spirit is life and peace;

[13] Galatians 5:22-23 – But the fruit of the Spirit is love, joy, peace, patience, kindness, goodness, faithfulness, gentleness and self-control. Against such things there is no law.

- Galatians 5:22-23 teaches us that love, joy, peace, patience, kindness, goodness, faithfulness, gentleness, and self-control are all indications that the Holy Spirit lives inside a person.

Achieving spiritual balance is critical. As Christians, we are called to love God with our whole beings and to love our neighbors as ourselves (Mark 12:30-31). In other words, we are called out of love to maintain a vertical relationship with God and a horizontal relationship with our neighbors. While both are important, the vertical must always come first.

A symbol of this balance is found in the cross. While both the vertical and horizontal planes are essential to the body of the cross, the vertical plane (the foundation) is longer than the horizontal plane. Certainly we must love and care for one another (horizontal plane), but our relationship with God is the most important (vertical plane).

It is good to help our neighbor and therefore contribute to the betterment of society. We cannot love God if we hate our neighbor, and we cannot love our neighbor and hate God. The love we have for our neighbor flows out of the relationship He first had with us. Only by God first loving us and placing his Spirit within us can we have a truly healthy relationship with our neighbor.

Therefore, go and do good deeds for your neighbor. However, do not neglect prayer, worship, and immersing yourself in the Word of God. These things will help you to maintain your own spiritual health so that you are able to establish an effective spiritual connection with others. By keeping the right balance, you can ensure yourself a healthy spiritual life.

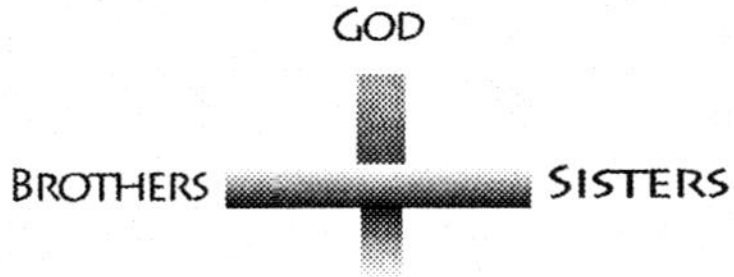

BALANCE

The first thing to remember about the mind, body, and spirit is that even though they all work together and are all valuable, they are not equally important. There needs to be balance within each area, but also between the three. While we seek balance in our physical life, in our mental life, and in our spiritual life, we also seek balance between these three lives. We do not balance them with equal weight, as the Chinese religion does with the Yin and Yang. The greatest emphasis should be placed on the spiritual life. I have learned over the years that the spirit influences the mind, and both the spirit and the mind influence our physical well-being.

First spirit, then mind, then body… keeping them in their proper order keeps your life on track. Most of the problems in people's lives can be traced back to improper sequence. Imagine someone who devotes 80% of his time building his body into a muscular machine and only 20% of his time shopping, eating, and doing other activities with family and friends. Now, imagine, the same body, mind, and spirit, but with a different balance structure. This person spends 30% of his time going to church and reading, 30% of his time training in the martial arts and doing other hobbies, and 40% of his time in relationships with friends, family, etc.

It doesn't take a Ph.D. to figure out that an identical body, mind, and spirit will be a very different person when the balance structure changes. For many of us, this is good news. It offers us a chance to become something new by simply changing the way we structure our lives. If the body builder didn't think it would change his body to do exercises and drink protein shakes, then he wouldn't bother. If the Christian didn't think that reading the Bible and going to Church would help him, then he wouldn't bother either. What it really comes down to is what we want out of life and what balance structure we will choose in order to obtain it.

1. Complete Self-Defense

Life Lesson: Self-defense is three-fold, and involves the body, mind, and spirit.

Self-defense is not just a term that applies to the body. When explaining this concept to a fellow martial artist, he questioned my use of the term self-defense in relation to the mind and spirit. His definition of self-defense was only of someone physically reacting to protect oneself or others in response to a harmful situation. I explained that my view of self-defense was more comprehensive. Mental, physical, and spiritual self-defense are all important in keeping safe, and taking preventative measures is crucial.

Protecting yourself against a physical attack is only necessary if a person is careless or unlucky enough to be in the wrong place at the wrong time, or if a person is targeted for other fleshly reasons such as revenge. Prevention is the key and demands training and preparation. Possessing good self-defense skills is about being ready for as many situations as possible. Although you can never be ready for everything, self-defense training will help you increase your readiness to handle a variety of potentially harmful situations.

Since self-defense is all about prevention, you don't have to wait until there is a physical threat in order to take action. In many cases, you can activate your mental and spiritual skills ahead of time to avoid physical defense. It is through mental and spiritual fitness that your overall street smarts for Christian martial arts will improve. Good martial artists use their minds as well as their spirits a lot more than they use their bodies in life-threatening situations.

Certainly, the ability to use the mind to think fast in dealing with a physical confrontation is important. However, confrontations are not always physical. The mind must also be sharp to defend against verbal and mental abuse. I'm not talking about being clever, quick-witted, or striking back with stinging remarks, as it is never appropriate to use verbal blows to hammer away at your opponent in the case of mental abuse. Even if an individual sinks low enough to try to cut you down by using abusive language, you should never stoop to his level and return fire. Words can be a powerful weapon that can cut deeper than any double-edged sword. Moreover, once that sword is swung, there is no taking it back. Sadly, the wounds inflicted can take a lifetime to heal.

So if mental sharpness in self-defense is not lashing back with putdowns, then how do you respond to verbal and mental abuse? As with the physical and spiritual, the real key is advance preparation. By building self-esteem and self-confidence, you construct a shield that deflects verbal blows. Nobody can make you feel bad about yourself without your internal permission. Although you may be called "stupid" by someone, it does no damage unless there is a piece of you that accepts it and believes it.

The most overlooked area of self-defense is spiritual. In our legal system, you will find that self-defense includes the right to protect those who cannot protect themselves from danger. Spiritually speaking, you and I fall into this category of being unable to protect ourselves. We are unable to protect ourselves from the eternal death and damnation caused by sin. While it is important that we train our spiritual nature, we must also understand that training can never aid us in winning the battle against sin.

No matter what we do, how good we get, or how hard we try, we will always fall short of the perfection necessary to get into Heaven. Luckily, we have Jesus, the ultimate self-defense master. He came to win the battle over sin and death. Notice that He did not come to protect Himself; He came to protect and save us. In the end, He saved us from the fatal blow of the devil. By believing in Jesus and placing our faith in His power, we can be assured of spiritual victory. It is only through this victory that we obtain the strength to train as Christian warriors in the mind and body.

Being connected to God the Father, through Jesus the Son, by the Holy Spirit, we indeed are plugged into a never-ending stream of power that carries us through danger. This power affects not only our spiritual lives, but our mental and physical lives, too. Through spiritual training, our mental and physical abilities heighten. We are better suited to handle conflict when it arises and defend others and ourselves against evil. Remember that advance preparation and the proper balance of mind, body, and spirit is the key. With adequate training, you will soon possess the self-defense skills necessary to keep you healthy in these three areas.

2. A Positive Response

Life Lesson: There are things that we choose and there are things that are chosen for us, but it's our attitude that determines our fate (and our altitude in that fate).

When new students come walking through my door, I often pose the question "Why are you here?" As you can imagine, I get a wide variety of responses. Most of the time, I hear things like, "For the exercise," "To learn self-defense," or "Just for fun." From kids, I'll occasionally hear, "Cuz my mom is making me," and in these instances, I feel sad and quite discouraged. People who are forced to be in class rarely do as well as those who make the choice. In fact, they usually end up wasting everyone's time.

Adults however are quite another story. I once had a student complain that I was forcing her to do pushups. I calmly explained that I could not force her to do anything. Considering that she weighed more than I did at the time, I don't believe I could have even picked her up let alone forced her to go through the motions of a pushup. I proceeded to inform her that although I was giving her direction, it was completely up to her as to whether or not she chose to follow it. After all, she walked through the door with her own free will, and her own free will kept her from walking right back out. Otherwise, she might as well have called me a kidnapper.

In our everyday lives, we are faced with countless choices. Believe it or not, we have a choice as to whether we want to work. We even have a choice as to whether we want to eat. Keep in mind that the latter may be dependent on the former. Consider those people who blame their misery on their job. It's probably not the job making them feel miserable, but rather, the attitude they carry about the job. After all, why don't they just quit? In all likelihood, their paycheck supports them and/or their family, but it's still their choice to be there.

The sooner we realize that the choices we make are ours, the sooner we can change our attitudes and make the best of them. Although Mr. Jones may not have the greatest job in the world, He can do one of two things under the present circumstances. He can complain every day and whine like a little baby, making himself and everyone around him unhappy, or he can look on the bright side, make the best of his job, and walk around with a positive and thankful attitude that pleases the Lord. After all, if he took time to think about it, that job is probably the source of many blessings.

Much like our Father in Heaven, we do not make choices haphazardly, we make them based on a careful set of goals and priorities, whether we realize it or not. This is one way we are made in the likeness of God. Consider that God made a choice to create and place us here on Earth because of the love that He has, and even more so because of the love that He is. He placed us in certain locations and with certain families for a reason. He did all of this knowing that we would make the choice to separate ourselves from Him by sinning, and therefore made another choice to sacrifice His one and only son to forgive and reunite us with Him.

Just as we do not enjoy many of the choices we make, God probably didn't enjoy the choice He made to sacrifice his one and only son on the cross. He probably also doesn't enjoy all the choices He makes in our individual lives. However, He did what He needed to do, and He does what He currently does, out of His love for us and His desire to put our needs ahead of His own comfort. Sometimes love is not all sweet and easy, as we well-know. Similarly, there are choices in our lives that we don't like making, and there are things that we don't like doing, but we do what we need to do for the greater good of ourselves and certain people that we love. Like God, we should do what we need to do with an attitude of love.

Whatever the circumstances may be, we can always ask ourselves "Why?" and make a healthy decision as to what we're going to think and do. While we may not be able to control everything that happens in our lives, we can accept and control what we ultimately make of what happens. Remember, our attitude determines our fate (and our altitude in that fate). Whining and moping usually doesn't get us very far, so there is no point in wasting our time on it. However, focusing on the blessings that God has given us, and realizing that our circumstances result in something greater than our own misery, can free us to soar to some magnificent high places.

3. Are You Too Busy?

Life Lesson: Life is not about time, it's about priorities.

More often than I've liked, I have felt it necessary deny martial arts promotions to students. This usually happens after I administer a test and discover that not all the requirements have been met; more specifically, students have not learned a particular series of movements or techniques that are crucial to the promotion. When I ask why, these students typically tell me that they didn't have time to practice. In other words, they were too busy.

As one of my black belts articulates, being too busy for something really means having different priorities. He once told the class about a time when he was working, going to school, pursuing a social life, and volunteering to teach karate. He was doing all these things and he still made time to practice. When I asked how he did it, he said that practicing was a priority for him, and that he sacrificed an extra hour of sleep every morning in order to work out.

Some people in his position might have said that they didn't have the time. He knew no such excuse. It was his choice to prioritize his life and do what needed to be done in order to accomplish his goals. Granted there are limits and not all of us always have the time and energy necessary to do everything we would like. However, our reserve of time, as well as physical and emotional energy, increases when we are motivated by our desires.

Subsequently, I am extremely cautious about telling others that I don't have time. I can't think of anything in my life that I don't have the time to do. However, I can think of many things that I don't make the time to do. For me, it is just a matter of priorities. For example, I remember when my Mom and I decided to take a day trip to Canada. We wanted to arrive at our destination by 8:00 AM, which meant I had to get up at 3:30. Looking back, I can hardly believe I was up that early. For something that was important to me, I was willing to sacrifice precious sleep.

What's truly incredible is that I was able to forgo my daily battle with the snooze button. Because I was excited about the trip, my eyes opened immediately and I found my feet hitting the floor almost as fast as the time it took my hand to reach over and silence the alarm. Of course, if you were to ask me why I haven't taken time to clean my garage in over a year, I would immediately respond, "I just don't have the time!" Perhaps a more appropriate response would be, "I choose not to make the time."

So far, I've only met one person whom I believe when he says, "I don't have the time." This individual is so busy that he puts my active schedule to shame. In fact, claiming that I have a schedule like his is like claiming that I play golf like Tiger Woods. There is simply no comparison! The man I'm talking about happens to be another one of my black belts by the name of Gary. Gary is an entrepreneur in the computer programming industry; he's a devoted husband, a loving father, and a faithful Christian and servant. I hold a great amount of respect for him… all because of the example that he sets in living his life.

Gary trains in the martial arts, plays on his church's softball league, teaches a Christian parenting class with his wife, serves as a leader in his church (occasionally preaching and often attending several meetings), remodels his house, plays with his kids, takes his wife out on dates, runs between five to ten miles daily, memorizes incredible amounts of scripture (whole books at time), writes a daily email devotion, councils struggling Christian brothers and sisters, evangelizes and witnesses to those who are not believers, and even drives hundreds of miles in one day to service clients from various cities. Okay, I'll admit he has told me that he often wakes up at 2 or 3 AM to accomplish all of this, but he has proven that anything is possible.

If anyone should be writing a book, it's definitely Gary (and I know he could find the time). This man's secrets to time management and discipline would be priceless to many. CEOs and presidents would pay thousands of dollars to fly him in to learn about his methods. However, even if he were to teach expensive seminars or write a book of his own, I'll save you the time and expense of having to see or read what he would tell you. I'll reveal his secret to you right now. Those things in his life are all priorities. He *MAKES* the time because they are important to him. Strangely enough, it seems to be the people who are the busiest who *have the time* to accomplish the most.

Many people say they don't attend church because of time. Believe me, I've been down that road myself. However, it's just an excuse to hide deeper issues that are going on inside. Whether it's a cry of not having time to do everything or a matter of the church service being too early, it still boils down to the fact that God is not a high enough priority. By choosing to place the Lord as number one in our lives, our spiritual self can grow and flourish. It can then properly influence the mental and physical self, allowing everything else to fall into place. Martin Luther used to say that the busier he was, the more reason he had to get up earlier and spend extra time in prayer. Now there's a man who had his priorities straight.

Luke 22:42[14] is about Jesus in the garden praying and contemplating the pain and torture that he will soon be going through. He indicates that His desire is for the burden to be taken from Him. Being God, He could have easily saved Himself; however, His greater desire was for His Father's will to be done. Furthermore, Jesus was putting humankind ahead of himself. He placed us, his children, ahead of his own comfort. As we learn from Jesus Christ, getting our priorities

---

[14] Luke 22:42 – Father, if you are willing, take this cup from me; yet not my will, but yours be done.

straight in life isn't always easy, but sometimes it's just plain necessary. I once heard of a great way to start; just think of JOY. To have true joy in life, our priorities should be ordered as follows: first Jesus, then Others and You.

I don't want or mean to say that *everyone* should be reprioritizing and making more time in life. However, I do want to say that *many* of us in today's society have our values mixed up. Some activities such as television watching, video gaming, etc. take our time and attention away from what should be our true priorities. While watching television and gaming can be fine activities, when done in excess, they prohibit us from engaging in necessary, positive, and more important activities.

My prayer is that as a society we will wake up and realize in what direction humanity is heading. We live in a culture that believes very firmly *it's all about me*, a culture that has its priorities reversed. Instead of promoting an intrinsic selfish attitude, we should be working towards an extrinsic outpouring of service. This is where Christians can do something to really help people. The more we move towards a world that promotes selflessness, the closer we move in the direction that the Lord desires for our lives. From a Christian perspective, this is getting our priorities straight and living out a life with purpose in Christ.

4. Mind Like Water

Life Lesson: It's the weeping willow that bends in a storm that best sustains the gusts of a strong wind.

The toughest part of learning to defend yourself is the uncertainty of situations you might find yourself in someday. Nobody knows the circumstances he/she might be confronted with when (God forbid that day should ever come) one may have to use physical martial arts skills to ward off an attacker. Will there be one assailant? Will there be two, or more? How big will they be? Will there be open space around, or will there be obstacles with which to contend? What will the terrain be like? Will there be help near by or not? Will a wallet appease the situation, or is the assailant after much more? The list of uncertainties is endless.

What then do I teach my martial arts students? I teach them to adapt to their surroundings. An ancient Japanese principle sums it up quite nicely; *Mizu No Kokoru* means, *mind like water*. Just as water in a stream is fluid enough to go around the boulder that lies in its path, we too should forego life's boulders. This applies to the physical principles of self-defense as well as adapting to one's environment. If an enemy who is much stronger throws a punch at us, we may not have the strength to stop it head on. However, deflecting it or redirecting its power might be within our abilities. Just keep in mind that every situation is different and our response must be flexible.

The methods in which we choose to defend ourselves vary entirely upon the situation. If it is wintertime and the sidewalk is icy, I probably wouldn't choose to lift my foot and kick, lest I fall on my rear end, become injured, and put myself in an even more compromising position. On the other hand, if my footing is firm and I need the extra reach and added power of a kick to defend myself against someone who is bigger than I am, I'll take full advantage of my legs any day of the week.

The intensity with which we choose to defend ourselves also depends on the situation. For example, if a drunken man means little harm by his offensive actions, certainly I wouldn't break his arm and strike him in the throat. Conversely, if I am backed into a corner and I believe that I'm going to be the victim of a stabbing, a medium punch to the stomach simply won't do. We must learn to adapt to each situation as it comes. We can learn from the chameleon that changes colors in harmony with its surroundings.

It would be nice if we knew what to prepare for in our day-to-day lives. Like self-defense, we never know what life has in store for us. The more flexible and adaptable we are to life's little surprises, the better our chances will be of making it through unscathed. If there is something in your life that you simply can't live without, step back and take a good hard look at it. Is it really that important? What would you do if something were to happen and you suddenly found yourself without it? Have you made provisions in your life and left room for a backup plan? Are your figurative insurance policies in place? Are all your eggs in one basket? Better yet, Are you holding just one egg?

After all, God created you to be adaptable. If you eat less over time, your stomach adapts and you begin to feel full with less food. Have you ever noticed that if you get 8-10 hours of sleep regularly, your body starts demanding it? If you are then forced to reduce those hours to 6-6 ½, your body adjusts and you don't feel tired anymore. So, be flexible and adaptable when necessary. Watch out for the blinders in life, which restrict you to the narrow path and keep you from fully discovering all the options at your doorstep. Remember, it's the weeping willow that bends easily in the storm that can best sustain the gusts of a strong wind. Are you ready to bend with opposition? Do you have the Mizu No Kokuro mindset in all aspects of your life?

In the Bible, Paul implies that he is the ultimate chameleon (1 Corinthians 9:19-23)[15]. His mind is truly like the water because it allows him to adapt to a wide variety of people and circumstances. Does he say that he believes whatever those around him believe? No. Are his principles and values wavering in the wind? Not at all! Paul stands firm on the Rock, which is Jesus Christ and doesn't budge from what he knows to be the Truth. He just molds the truth differently and presents it in a way that different people and cultures can understand. This takes a deep understanding of people and how they are moved to action.

To acquire a mind like water, it is necessary to pay close attention to your surroundings until you develop a keen sense of awareness about where you are and who is around you. Only by understanding an environment can you know how to best adapt to a situation it presents. As you embark on this journey, perceive but don't assume, plan but don't worry, and always be open to learn new things. It is possible to be pliable without being spineless. In doing so, you'll be open to greater possibilities. Only when the chameleon achieves true understanding of the leaf, can it turn that color, become one with its surroundings, and achieve true harmony. Doing so saves its life!

---

[15] 1 Corinthians 9:19-23 – Though I am free and belong to no man, I make myself a slave to everyone, to win as many as possible. To the Jews I became like a Jew, to win the Jews. To those under the law I became like one under the law (though I myself am not under the law), so as to win those under the law. To those not having the law I became like one not having the law (though I am not free from God's law but am under Christ's law), so as to win those not having the law. To the weak I became weak, to win the weak. I have become all things to all men so that by all possible means I might save some. I do all this for the sake of the gospel, that I may share in its blessings.

5. Where is Your Focus?

Life Lesson: Wherever you are, it's in your best interest to be there in body, mind, and spirit.

Class is ready to begin, and students are scattered throughout the room, engaged in various activities. Some are practicing; some are stretching and warming up; and some are gabbing with friends. Others are still adjusting their uniforms or walking through the door. While there's a lot of activity going on, none of it looks like a disciplined martial arts class. "Line up," the instructor barks firmly, and in a mad flurry, students scurry to their designated places in rows. What was unorganized and lacking in structure a short time ago has suddenly transformed into sleek, regimented, straight lines of students awaiting the instructor to breathe his next command.

The beginning of martial arts class is actually quite amazing, distractions disappear, and the only thing that exists for the next hour is the class. This is the martial way of focusing 100% on our training. Shutting out distractions is not ignoring them; it's focusing on the task at hand. We can all accomplish so much more by being present (in mind and spirit, as well as in body). It seems silly, but saying "wherever you are, be there" holds great meaning. Whatever you find yourself doing, whether you chose to be there, or you have no choice but to be there, you might as well make the best of it. Focus on what you are doing, put forth your greatest effort, shut out all distractions, and concentrate.

From a training stance, focus is directing all of one's energy into a clear target. More specifically, it's driving one's energy into a bull's eye. Think of the difference between the complete, whole area of the fist hitting a target, versus just one or two knuckles making contact with a specific point. When the whole fist reaches its destination, the force is dissipated or spread out over a wider striking surface; little damage is done, and not much is accomplished. However, when just one or two knuckles hit, all of the force penetrates into one specific point. Now, the blow is powerful. Instead of wasting energy, optimal results are achieved and the impact is greater. This is true in all of life; when we are present in body, mind, and spirit, results are much greater and better.

Focus is especially important in spiritual warfare. While we may not always be in mental turmoil, and may never face strenuous physical battles, spiritual battles are fought and lives are at stake daily! Satan and his minions are continually looking for ways in which to disrupt our lives and pull us away from our walk with the Lord. Distractions are being thrown into our path to make us stumble, fall, and turn away from God. Some people have many and others have few, but we all deal with distractions on some level. If we can follow the Apostle Paul's instructions to think about and set our minds on whatever is true, noble, right, pure, lovely, admirable, excellent, and praiseworthy (Philippians 4:8)[16], distractions will run out the back door.

A high degree of focus is only developed with much time and training. Its workout partner is discipline and the two make an inseparable team. If you possess the discipline to persevere, like the way in which doing pushups becomes easier over time, then focus will come to you with less effort. Begin by focusing on simple tasks and learn how easy they can become if mind, body, and spirit are engaged. Next, discipline yourself to work through tasks that seem daunting or even burdensome. This training will build you up and make you stronger. Soon those tasks that seem daunting and burdensome will become less taxing. Eventually you will get to the point where focusing is second nature and actually becomes a ready and available tool which serves you well.

---

[16] Philippians 4:8 – Finally, brothers, whatever is true, whatever is noble, whatever is right, whatever is pure, whatever is lovely, whatever is admirable–if anything is excellent or praiseworthy–think about such things.

6. Get Back in Stance

Life Lesson: True success can only be found on the far side of failure.

Often times, the first impression I have of people as I talk to them about joining my martial arts classes is that they are afraid of appearing imperfect. I hear things like "I want to get in better shape before I join," or "I'd try it, but I don't think I'd be any good." This tells me that people aren't afraid of martial arts, but rather of making a fool of themselves by appearing unable or unknowing in their practice of martial arts. Because they don't want to appear imperfect, and don't feel comfortable making mistakes, they don't even try.

It is human nature to disguise our imperfections and cover up our mistakes. We wear masks daily because we are ashamed of ourselves as imperfect beings. The challenge comes in removing the masks. Even though we know in our hearts that we're imperfect, it appeases us to ignore this fact. In other words, it appeases us to think and act as if we are perfect like God, even though we're not. It is only when we can recognize and accept ourselves as imperfect sinners that we can begin to find comfort with who we are and admit to others and to ourselves what truly is within us.

As we're training in martial arts class, I tell students that it is okay to make mistakes. I also tell them to get comfortable with not knowing everything and not being perfect because our imperfections aren't going away. As a matter of fact, learning can only occur when we are open to possible failure. It takes courage to risk goofing up in the pursuit of knowledge. If we spend all our time putting on a façade by pretending to know it all at the sacrifice of learning, then we miss all the beautiful things that God has to offer us through life. Willingness to make mistakes is a valuable trait that a wise martial artist will foster.

.en we get frustrated, embarrassed, angry, or upset , of mistakes we make, our minds become clouded, ,udgment is hindered, and our direction is lost. Instead of ,arning, we waste valuable time and energy worrying about our image and trying to cover up our error. This effort to protect our image by covering up our mistakes is merely a distraction that keeps us from completing the task at hand. It can be thought of as a chain reaction, a domino effect, or a snowball rolling down a hill. As the snowball picks up speed and mass when it travels down a hill, one out-of-control area of our lives can pick up and affect other areas and before we know it, everything is in chaos.

Because all areas of life are interconnected, and one area will always have an effect on another, we must stop the snowball effect before it's too late and everything comes crashing on top of us. Remember, an ounce of prevention is worth a pound of cure. As Christian martial artists, we must train ourselves to think defensively in a Christian way. When a mistake is made, the wise martial artist will accept the consequences, learn, and move forward. For he knows that learning, and pressing on, is more important that getting wrapped up in fruitless endeavors like making excuses.

Just as we must find peace with mistakes in our own lives, we must extend peace to others, too. People who are intolerant of other's mistakes usually have not found it within themselves to allow mistakes of their own. These people are sometimes overly critical and self-righteous, and they have not yet removed the masks with which they hide. I find it curious that people who make fun of others and feel the need to put others down often don't think highly of themselves deep down inside. Degradation becomes the spring of water by which their thirst for self-esteem is temporarily satisfied. It is only through actual self-esteem and true self-comfort that a person's thirst can become quenched in order to rise up and forgive others.

So how do we become comfortable with ourselves? We stop looking for our identity, security, and meaning through our image and seek these things from God. If we look to God for our total fulfillment, we can rest easy that He'll never let us down. If our identity is first in being a child of God, then there is no more pressure for us to put on a façade and pretend that we're perfect as He is. For Christ died precisely for this reason...to conquer all of our imperfections and sin. Through Him, we have victory and we are made perfect. We only need to learn to die to ourselves. This can be practiced by taking risks with our self-image and allowing ourselves to make mistakes now and again. In Him, our focus shifts and we can live free and unencumbered by fear of failure. In Him, we fail, but we also succeed.

7. Submission and Authority

Life Lesson: Submission and authority go hand in hand, working together to sift the sand.

A common thread that you'll find in many martial arts schools is the use of some sort of ranking system. Usually it's a color scheme of belts or sashes that helps to distinguish the skill levels of one student from another. There are many reasons for using ranking systems: allowing students to see tangible progress of short-term goals, building confidence and self-esteem through accomplishments, teaching submission and respect as a way to develop learning skills, and granting responsibilities and privileges as a way to develop teaching skills. Ranking systems can be quite valuable to the learning process that occurs in martial arts.

The exchange that occurs between the ranks is an interesting learning dynamic. The low ranking student learns how to perform from the high-ranking student, and the high-ranking student learns how to teach from the low ranking student. In essence, the low ranking student learns through submission and the high-ranking student learns through authority (or service). Submission is the key for the dynamic to occur. If submission is missing, then learning cannot take place and both parties might as well go home. After all, a glass cannot be filled before it has been emptied. Far too often, students expect to learn from the teacher, but are unwilling to submit or empty themselves to be filled.

God also wants us to empty ourselves in order to receive all He has to offer. Paul told Timothy that if we purge ourselves of impurities, we will be useful to the Master (2 Timothy 2:20-21)[17]. Purging can be accomplished through

[17] 2 Timothy 2:20-21 – In a large house there are articles not only of gold and silver, but also of wood and clay; some are for noble purposes and some for ignoble. If a man cleanses himself from the latter, he will be an

confession and absolution (1 John 1:9)[18]. Paul obviously knew what he was talking about because God chose him for a great purpose and used him in mighty ways. Consider what God told Ananias about Paul being His chosen instrument (Acts 9:15)[19]. God used these men in mighty ways and He can use you, too. However, you must be clean, and you must be empty for Him to transform you into His vessel.

Many students don't submit because they are under the misconception that submitting to someone or something is self-degrading. A stranger once told me about an experience he had working for a hotel. When he was hired, his supervisor told him to use the servants' entrance in the back, instead of the front door. He told his supervisor that he and his hotel could go and... (I'll censor the rest of his sentence). Clearly, he was angry at the notion of being treated like a servant. However, his use of course language also told me that he was trying to protect his self-image by appearing tough and unwilling to submit to the hotel's rules. I must have come across as a real wimp when I told him that I was in a similar situation once and didn't see anything wrong with not using the front door.

Husbands and wives, parents and children, children and teachers, employees and employers, landlords and tenants, and customers and businesses all relate through submission and authority. Consider the traditional vows of marriage. Some women have a problem with the "love, honor, and *obey*" the husband because they think it means the husband is the boss and the wife is the slave. If that's what a

---

instrument for noble purposes, made holy, useful to the Master and prepared to do any good work.

[18] 1 John 1:9 – If we confess our sins, he is faithful and just and will forgive us our sins and purify us from all unrighteousness.

[19] Acts 9:15 – But the Lord said to Ananias, "Go! This man is my chosen instrument to carry my name before the Gentiles and their kings and before the people of Israel."

woman thinks about obeying her husband, then she's not seeing the whole picture. Yes, women are called by God to submit to their husbands, as the husband is the head of the family (Ephesians 5:22-24)[20]. However, husbands are also called to serve their wives. The reality is that both parties are called to support each other through mutual submission (Ephesians 5:21)[21].

God instructs husbands to love their wives as they love their own bodies (Ephesians 5:28a)[22]. Moreover, God commands husbands to love their wives as Christ loves His Church (Ephesians 5:25)[23]. As we all know, Christ gave up everything for His bride, the Church. He put her first and even gave His life for her when the time came. In the same way, husbands too are called to give their lives for their wives. The husband-wife relationship is the second greatest example of how authority is actually a form of service. The greatest example is of course the sacrifice that Christ made on the cross.

While the concept of marriage is far from martial arts training, it does help us to understand proper authority in relationship to submission. Submission isn't all bad and authority isn't all good. Those people who are in authority have a responsibility to listen and respond to the thoughts and feelings of their followers. If they don't, then the relationship will be dysfunctional. It's a common mistake for a leader to

---

[20] Ephesians 5:22-24 – Wives, submit to your husbands as to the Lord. For the husband is the head of the wife as Christ is the head of the church, his body, of which he is the Savior. Now as the church submits to Christ, so also wives should submit to their husbands in everything.

[21] Ephesians 5:21 – Submit to one another out of reverence for Christ.

[22] Ephesians 5:28a – In this same way, husbands ought to love their wives as their own bodies.

[23] Ephesians 5:25 – Husbands, love your wives, just as Christ loved the church and gave himself up for her.

believe that he has been put in a position of power to simply dictate and reap personal rewards. Leaders tend to forget that they were appointed to *lead* through servitude. It's when leaders don't understand their role that they become useless and abuse their power. In fact, several leaders throughout history have experienced their downfall due to an inability or unwillingness to serve.

Leaders serve their followers in many ways. They must serve in order to lead! It's unfortunate that much of this service goes on unrecognized and sometimes unappreciated. My martial arts school is just one example. I often hear people remark about how awesome it must be to be the master of a martial arts school. After all, they see me giving orders to people in class, running things as I please, putting students through grueling and painful exercises, exercising authority to promote or demote students, and receiving monetary payment from people to let me take control of their lives to some degree. What they don't realize is all the sacrifices I make in the process.

First, there's the expense. If run in a traditional way, it is extremely tough to make a martial arts school lucrative. Consider the investment and risk of thousands upon thousands of dollars out of a small business owner's pocket for start-up costs. Advertising, utilities, rent, taxes, repairs, training, and safety equipment are just the beginning. I can tell you from personal experience and 25 years of observing other martial arts school owners, it is rare to do more than break even. In fact, I know of many instructors who use income from their second (and yes even third) jobs in order to support their schools.

In addition to the expense, running a school takes a lot of time. Realistically speaking, time is probably the biggest sacrifice that the instructor makes on the account of others. The head instructor is often the janitor, maintenance worker, bookkeeper, and secretary, in addition to being the big boss. Consider the time such instructors spend away from family and friends. Think about the yards that go un-mowed and the garages that go un-cleaned. I assure you that their time is probably worth much more than the net income they receive from running their martial arts schools.

Last but not least, there's the sacrifice of talent. When identifying the heroes of martial arts, most people pick out Bruce Lee, Chuck Norris, and Jackie Chan. However, I'd also like to encourage you to give recognition to the everyday instructors who work behind the scenes; those that give all they've got so that others can get ahead and shine in the spot light. These instructors sometimes possess just as much talent as super stars that are well known. The difference is that instead of pursuing fortune and fame, they choose to sacrifice their own advancement to teach and train others.

All of these sacrifices are ways that instructors serve their students. They place their students above themselves in terms of priority. Actually, many people willfully submit to others in this way. Consider our President. Some children say that they'd like to grow up to be President; however, I'm sure they'd reconsider that if they understood all the sacrifices our President makes. He forever sacrifices a normal social life. He is forever at risk and in fear of attack. The survival of every living thing on this planet could be in jeopardy if he says or does the wrong thing. Our nation's stability and future is in his hands. No thank you! I wouldn't want all that weight on my shoulders. And that's just one example.

I thank God every day that we have people who are ready, willing, and able to serve this country in all sorts of capacities. In fact, we should all stop and give thanks for soldiers in the military because they're a great example of people who give of themselves to serve. Some even give their lives. The military is truly one of the finest examples of submission that I can imagine. Similar to martial arts, people work their way up in rank through a powerful relationship between followers and leaders that promotes teamwork and success.

So who answers to whom in life? If you say everyone answers to each other, that followers and leaders work together in an interdependent relationship where no one person receives 100% of the benefits, then you're well on your way to unlocking the secret to a happier and healthier life. What it all boils down to is that none of us is on a one-way street of rank and importance in this world. We all have a part to play. We all fit together, not just in a row or a vertical line with those on the top benefiting from those on the bottom. It's more like an interdependent network all intertwined to support and feed back into one another.

How do we all work together? Not through selfish ulterior motives. You see, it's not true submission or authority if we are focused on the ways in which we will benefit in the long term; it's just greed and selfishness disguised in servant's clothing. True submission and authority is a selfless act of keeping other people's needs ahead of our own. If you focus on what you can give in a relationship, and not on what you can out of it, you'll appreciate the benefits more. The right balance of submission and authority is the key to the love that God meant for every one of us to share. Both are service-oriented and both are dependent on each other.

8. Quality Before Quantity

Life Lesson: If you're going to do something, do it right or don't do it at all.

During the first month that students join a martial arts class, they go through some hard times. If they're going to drop, this is usually when it occurs. One contributing factor to the high percentage of dropouts is that students usually feel overwhelmed by all that there is to do and learn. Besides feeling overwhelmed and overworked, students don't feel as if they're accomplishing much right off the bat. Frustration sets in and many beginners feel as if they are failing.

Martial arts instructors attempt to deal with this transition period by helping students to develop short-term goals, giving them positive reinforcement, and managing their expectations from a realistic point of view. This doesn't mean that martial arts instructors lower their standards or expectations of students. If we were to water down our standards and allow people to move on without truly having the correct techniques, I'm sure you'd agree that we'd be doing them a great disservice.

Imagine thinking that what you are doing is correct and so you continue to practice it that way time and again. Many years go by and it becomes second nature. Then, all of the sudden, you learn that you've been doing it incorrectly. Oh my! As you can imagine, it's a lot better to take your time and make sure what you're doing is correct before moving on to the next level. Otherwise, you have a lot of backtracking to do. Just remember, quality before quantity. If quality is your primary focus, quantity will progress on its own.

Training a martial artist is like building a high-rise tower. Without a strong foundation, your entire complex is weak. You could have the strongest eighth floor that man has ever seen, but if your first floor collapses, the strength and beauty of the eighth floor was all for nothing. It is sometimes agonizing and takes patience and endurance to get something right before moving on, but in the long term, its well worth it. Cutting corners and taking shortcuts will help you feel good in the short term, but only give you headaches in the end.

Along these lines, I teach my students to do things right or don't do them at all. If exercises or techniques are done incorrectly, they can have very negative consequences. That's why I tell folks to work hard, but at their own pace. If we're doing pushups and some students can't do as many as those who have had years of training, then they should only do their best. Instead of doing twice as many pushups the wrong way, they should do half as many pushups the right way. It's safer and results come faster and stronger.

The same thing applies to all things we learn in life. Character and temperament are formed within a child's first few years of life. The environment in which a child is placed throughout the early years of his or her life will play a crucial role in who this child becomes and what he or she does in adulthood. Once poor habits, patterns, and other negative tendencies are established, it takes twice the energy to correct them than it would have taken to formulate positive attitudes and behaviors right from the beginning.

A force in motion is extremely difficult to stop. This is why I suggest always giving your best from the start. Overcoming destructive behavior is possible, it's just difficult to accomplish. If you've discovered you didn't do or get something right before moving on, don't be too discouraged because there's hope. With a strong enough counter force, its momentum can be slowed, stopped, and even turned around. It's definitely not easy, but you can do anything (Philippians 4:13)[24] to which you set your mind!

Now apply these simple steps: first and foremost, build on a solid foundation; work at your own pace; make a plan and set short-term goals that will lead to your long-term

---

[24] Philippians 4:13 – I can do everything through Him who gives me strength.

goals; become proficient at step one of the goal before you move on to step two; surround yourself with people who encourage you and build you up; have confidence in yourself; learn to forgive yourself if you do end up making a mistake (or two); and above all, do your best right from the start! Also, understand that behavioral inertia can be redirected if you put forth the effort.

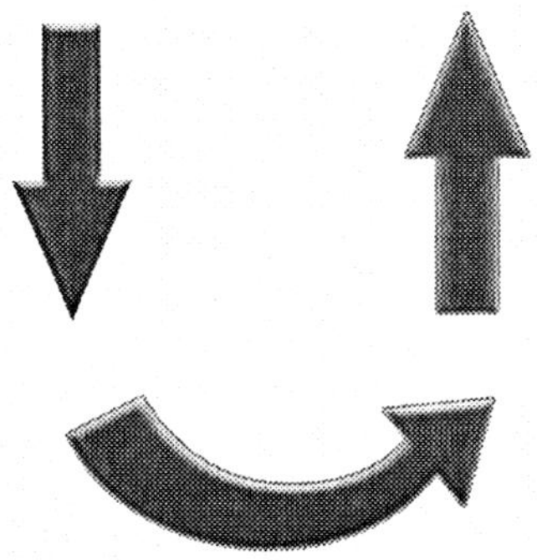

9. Two Ears and One Mouth

Life Lesson: Before venturing to speak, be still and listen.

When it comes to martial arts, I've discovered over the years that parents usually have very different goals than their young children. Young children often come to karate class because they want to mimic all the physical movements that they see on television and in the movies. Their parents on the other hand are usually focused on the rigid structure, mental discipline, and behavioral modifications that are associated with the martial arts, as well as the high levels of respect that students possess.

While most parents understand that martial arts help to develop desirable qualities in children, they don't stop to think about how. Bowing is a prime example. It is common to think of the Eastern bow as equivalent to the Western handshake. However, it's more than a mere greeting; it's a sign of respect, which really translates into good manners. Good manners aren't only important for tradition's sake; they facilitate interaction between you and the people you meet.

As an instructor, one of the biggest areas I focus on is good manners, or how students communicate respect to other students and instructors. Hence, I developed four rules that I ask students to follow:

1. Don't interrupt others! Now, if I'm in the middle of a sentence and the building is burning down without my knowledge, then please, by all means, feel free to interject a "pardon me, Master Brown." However, short of an emergency, students sometimes need to practice the old ancient art of keeping their mouths shut. This is especially true of the very young. One example might be when I'm in the middle of explaining something, and instead of listening intently, there's a little kid that just can't wait to

tell me about the zebra that he saw at the zoo the other day. This is why we have rules about raising our hands before we speak. Students in the classroom know that when they raise their hands, it's either to answer a question or to ask one. For the most part, we all need to learn to listen when someone else is speaking. Listening makes us a lot smarter than speaking. Someone once said that God gave us two ears but only one mouth because He wanted us to spend twice as much time listening as we spend talking and because He knew listening was twice as difficult.

2. Answer respectfully. Not only do we encourage using "yes" as a response in lieu of "ya," "yup," "uh-huh," or "mmm-hmm," for respectful purposes, but also it makes for much clearer communication skills. You'll be surprised at how many more misunderstandings are avoided when you begin answering folks clearly and specifically.

3. Answer the question asked. I can't tell you how many times I'll ask someone a question like, "Did you move the stapler off my desk?" and their response is to begin telling me a long and drawn out tale of how they had this English paper due for school and their mom was late picking them up for class because she had a tough day at... STOP ALREADY! Please just answer the question. It was intended to invoke a simple "yes" or "no" response. Obviously, direct answers may not be appropriate if you are in a social situation where short responses are considered rude. The key is to be able to recognize what is appropriate for each individual setting.

4. Don't make excuses; just say yes and thank you. This one is a close cousin to number three and is especially true for those that have a hard time admitting their faults and/or allowing others to think that they're capable of making

mistakes. If this is you, then relax and stop with the charade because everyone knows that you're not perfect. Nobody is perfect, so when people give you a suggestion, comment, or maybe some direction, don't start defending yourself. Just say yes, indicate that you understand, and thank them for their input. A "thank you" in response to input lets people know that you recognize their intentions as good. It invites clear communication and opens up the channels for further dialogue. Defending yourself by trying to justify your behavior sends the message that you're either insecure or so full of yourself that you can't admit error. Remember that it's a true friend who will tell another that he is walking around with a piece of lunch still lingering in his beard when others either laugh and talk behind his back for their own amusement, or just completely ignore him all together. Therefore, be grateful when someone gives you instruction or corrects your behavior with the proper attitude. It's a bold step to risk conflict or a feeling of discomfort in order to help someone. Nobody but a friend would waste the time.

Now before you begin thinking that I consider myself high and mighty, let me tell you that I'm just as guilty as the next person for breaking my own rules. One downfall of mine is remembering people's names. This is a prime symptom of not listening to others. It just seems that when I meet someone, it takes me at least three or four times of re-meeting her before I can get her name in my brain. The problem is that I'm too wrapped up in my own thoughts and feelings, and worrying about what she thinks of me.

More often than not, I find that when I meet other people, I'm wrapped up in whether or not they hear my name correctly, or that I make a good first impression. I'm usually looking for them to understand what a great person I am, or at least I want it to appear that way. Why do I want to appear better than I am? I reckon it's because of insecurities deep down inside. Nonetheless, if I could just manage to stop believing that it's all about me, then I could focus solely on the other person and really listen.

Jesus Himself set an excellent example in this area. He truly knew the verse "Be still and know that I am God" (Psalm 46:10a). In fact, we find examples spread throughout the ministry of Jesus about how He made time for the Father in His schedule. Indeed, He even made spending time with God a crucial part of His normal routine. Jesus also made time for people and always met their needs. He really knew people, and he healed, encouraged, and comforted them. He really knew how to listen, which is the beginning step in accomplishing such things.

Jesus had a deep, intimate, and strong relationship with His Father in Heaven. As we all know, relationships are dependent on communication, and communication is a two-way vehicle. I imagine Jesus spent hours upon hours just relaxing, hanging out, and being still with His Dad, and He didn't do all the talking either. Too many of us are caught up in praying and talking to God and don't take time to listen to Him. Like Jesus, I urge you to take plenty of regular time listening to God. Of course, He wants to hear you, too. Just don't dominate the conversation!

God went to a lot of trouble to ensure a medium by which we could communicate daily. So join me in an endeavor to turn away from being self-absorbed and truly listen to what our Creator has to say. Don't focus so much on what you're going to say to Him and listen to what He has to say to you. The Bible tells us to be still so that we can listen! In the spiritual world, prayer is how we speak and being still is how we listen. Both are important and both are necessary for true communication to occur.

10. Who Made You Do It?

Life Lesson: Taking responsibility for your own actions will take you far in life.

One of the principles of martial arts is responsibility. In my classes, one facet of being responsible means taking care of your own possessions. Beginners find out quickly that items left at the karate school become the property of the instruct-tors. This isn't some attempt at picking on the new person; it's an attempt to teach the scatter-brained about focus. I eagerly make it known that property can be purchased back at any time, but not with money. Payment is usually made in the form of pushups. Allowing students to associate a conse-quence with their undesirable behavior is helpful in keeping the behavior from occurring again.

Of course, the concept of responsibility extends far beyond taking care of our things. It is also about taking care of our actions. Has anyone ever *made you* do something? While people do make other people do things by way of force, most of us are guilty of using this phrase with great exaggeration. Let's face it, even in the case of a knife or gun being held to us, we still have choices. Life is full of choices and we make them every day. There are some choices that are inconsequential, and there are others that have long lasting effects on the rest of our lives.

It's not that I don't understand the term "he/she made me" as a figure of speech; it's that I want to instill a mindset that we are in control of our choices. We are responsible for the things we say and do. In the martial arts, I usually assoc-iate this more with student's physical actions (specifically when fighting is the issue). I make it very clear, in no uncertain terms, that I do not tolerate fighting, except in the case of extreme emergencies where self-defense is the last resort. If someone is being picked on, there are usually wiser choices than resorting to violence.

We all need to be responsible for ourselves. I go to great lengths to teach this principle to young people and to their parents. When a parent of one of my young people simply can't step back and let the student do the learning, there's a potential problem. I make it a rule that if children are old enough to be in my class, then they are old enough to be responsible. If a child misbehaves, the child is punished, not the parent. If a child has a question, the child needs to learn to ask, not the parent. Of course, it would be ridiculous to expect an eight year old to discuss the terms of his annual contract with me. However, I most certainly would expect an eight year old to ask me how to tie his belt.

It's my job to teach communication and responsibility, because learning these skills is important in the growth and development of a martial artist. In some instances, I have parents that actually join class and participate with their kids. However, they are usually a little dismayed when I separate them by pairing parents up with parents and kids up with kids. If the class is doing something as a group, I'll even go to the trouble to put family members on the opposite sides of the room. I let the parents know right away that they are not in class to hold their child's hand. Anyway, it's usually the parent's hand that needs to be held more often than the child's, due to the parent's difficulty in letting go and allowing the child to be more independent.

I actually wish that I could get more parents to begin studying with me. I've run across many who could use a few lessons in self-responsibility. In just the first ten years of running my martial arts business, customers intentionally reneged and left owing me a combined total of more than thirty-thousand dollars that to this day I've never recovered. Incredible! It's not the thought of the money that floors me; it's the thought of all these people having no sense of obligation or responsibility for their actions. I'm not counting the people who knew they couldn't pay and had the decency to speak with me about it. I gave a lot of credit to those folks (literally and figuratively).

I finally was so fed up with people who stiffed me for their bills, that I began using collection agencies and the legal system to enforce payments. You wouldn't believe the reactions I got from most people. Most of them were actually angry with me and shocked that I would pursue collection. Some were even hostile. Over the years I allowed plenty of these relationships go south over money. It reached a point that it just wasn't worth it anymore. I eventually moved into the non-profit direction and began accepting donations en lieu of a fee from everyone who participated in my classes. No more struggles with people over finances, no more broken relationships, and no more going crazy over the irresponsible actions of those who refused to live up to their obligations.

To me, it's mind-boggling to even imagine not paying a debt that I owe. I have been late paying bills of my own, but I at least send in something to show good faith. At the beginning of running my business, there were many times when I would walk in the door and flick on the lights with hesitancy. Was I going to have electricity that day? Was there still a dial tone on the phone? Had the utility company cancelled my service yet? I did three things during these trying times. First, I got my priorities straight and cut whatever expenses weren't necessary. Second, I paid something every month to all the companies I owed. Third, if I owed money to personal acquaintances, I was mature enough to speak with them about it, keep them apprised of my situation, and tell them when I could pay them back.

Unfortunately, this issue of responsibility isn't limited to martial arts classes. I see case after case of young adults with accountability issues. Whatever happened to the day when you spilled a cup of coffee on yourself and didn't sue the restaurant for not warning you that it would be hot? Believe it or not, there was a time when a person fell down the stairs and was simply embarrassed for being clumsy. Now we want to hold someone else accountable for everything bad that happens to us and for anything in our lives that we don't like. If we get ourselves into too much debt, it's the credit card company's fault for allowing us to borrow so much money. If we make bad choices in life, then it's our parent's fault for not raising us perfectly. As a society, we have twisted "life, liberty, and the pursuit of happiness" into "life, liberty, and the right to be happy." I even heard of a lawsuit recently where a person sued the school he attended for not giving him a proper education.

People are even saying their own failure is not their fault! Certainly, it is disappointing to fail, but it happens to all of us and we should learn how to face it, accept it, and take it for what it's worth. Failure actually has value for success. Winston Churchill said, "Success is about going from failure to failure without loss of enthusiasm." Even Confucius said, "Our greatest glory is not in never falling but in rising every time we fall." Freedom from failure means freedom from success. Imagine the pride and feeling of self-worth that millions of people are missing today because their actions are not their own. Instead, we have insecure undisciplined people who can't take care of themselves. Imagine the peace and low crime there could be if everyone experienced consequences from their own actions.

On a more positive note, there are plenty of people who are responsible and accountable. These people wouldn't expect others to carry their burdens. I've had the honor and privilege of meeting a significant number of people in my life whose characters are impeccable. However, I do see a tendency in our country to lean in the opposite direction. There are definitely more self-centered people today than there were just a generation or two ago. Certainly, I don't pretend to have all the answers; however, I do know that working together as a team and placing our faith in the One who does have all the answers is the only sure bet we have. So let us pray and place all confidence in God's hands.

11. Perception or Reality?

Life Lesson: How we interpret reality depends on the light we use to perceive it.

A crucial skill in martial arts is the ability to perceive things as they truly are, despite many distractions and façades that can lead us astray. While acquiring this skill is often a slow process, it can keep us out of harms way and possibly even save our lives. For example, how would you respond to someone verbally attacking you? Would you simply turn your back and walk away or would you use your martial arts techniques? If you decided that you would use your martial arts techniques, which ones would you use? Well, it depends on the circumstances. There is never only one solution when it comes to life and death.

You might think it's logical to walk away, but your *spidey sense* (for all you comic book fans) is telling you that there is real danger present. After all, you could be jumped from behind. Some criminals know and use tricks to weaken your defense just before they attack. In fact, I once knew a sport karate fighter who ran his mouth to get the best of others. He used putdowns (ones that often struck a nerve), off-the-wall phrases, silly noises, and anything else he could think of to throw his opponent off guard. When we were sparring, he knew that it would be much easier to *clean my clock*[25] if he could stir up my emotions. He knew that if I were frustrated or angry then my body and mind would both become rigid and I wouldn't be able to react quickly enough.

When we are agitated or upset about something, it's tough to keep things in their proper perspective. With just one fighter whom I hardly knew, I had to continually remind myself that there was a bigger picture. In order for me to be victorious, I had to take his words with a grain of salt and

---

[25] Clean my clock – an expression that means my opponent desires to take his hands and feet and beat the ever-living snot right out of my head. ☺

recognize them for what they were…a mere distraction. People can cause quite a stir by distracting and throwing us off our game if we're not careful. Self-defense (and life in general) is all about keeping things in proper perspective. It's prioritizing. Ask yourself this question, what's the most important thing you should focus on for whatever it is that you need to accomplish? In other words, do you really need to worry about being called nasty names, when you know its only intention is to distract you? After all, you may have the larger issue of a knife in your attacker's hand.

Let's say that you find yourself alone in a dark place where nobody can hear you scream for help. Now, I know that you wouldn't place yourself in such a situation, but for the sake of this example, please humor me. Suddenly, without any warning, a thief steps out from around a corner with a weapon and tells you to hand over your valuables. What do you do? Well, two questions must be asked before making a decision. First, are the things you are carrying more valuable than your life? Second, under what circumstances (if any) do you think the assailant will allow you to walk away without harm? In other words, will the things that you have on your person actually appease this thug, or do you think he's after something more?

If you truly believe that nothing you can peacefully give up will ultimately stop you from being seriously hurt, then my advice is certainly to begin weighing your options of a physical defense. Most of the time this will probably not be the case. In the majority of instances, my recommendation would be for you to hand over the items demanded with no hesitation or resistance. This poses a problem for some people whose entire existence revolves around *stuff.* Erich Fromm said, "If I am what I have, and if I lose what I have, who then am I?" Although I'll admit that some stuff is important, what it comes down to is priorities. Your safety and the safety of others must always come first.

Looking for my first piece of real estate was quite a challenge. After an incredible amount of time and effort, I finally found a seller that was willing to work with me on my payments by allowing me to move in and pay him directly on a land contract arrangement. The payments I had to make in order to own this building were equal to the amount of money I was already paying every month in rent. Since I was only nineteen at the time, and my lack of credit only superseded my lack of cash, I didn't see how I could refuse the deal. I hadn't yet established enough credit, the banks wouldn't give me the time of day, and I wasn't in favor of borrowing money from a guy named Lefty.

I remember when I picked up the keys to the new place. Our current karate school was only a couple of blocks down the street and I was holding classes that night with a bunch of my most faithful students. After class, I decided to bring them down the street to see their new school. Keep in mind that the place was a *fixer-upper* to say the least. After all, you get what you pay for, and I wasn't paying much! It was full of trash; the walls were literally crumbling down in places; there wasn't any water in the building (except what was deposited from the leaking roof), and people had actually been using the basement floor as a place to relieve themselves of their human waste. Yes, it was bad, and when we arrived at the front door, the students stood with their mouths agape in unbelief.

My students actually thought I was joking around, until I pulled the keys out my pocket and proceeded to walk in the door. To them, I was crazy, and the structure was the most horrible thing they had ever laid their eyes on. However, to me, I was making a wise investment and the building had lots and lots of potential for improvement. To me, trash and filth was an easy problem to fix, which just required a little elbow grease. It was the walls and the roof that presented the real challenges. I eventually put up faux walls in front of the crumbling ones, and left strict instructions to the students not to ever lean up against them in certain areas. The problem wasn't solved; it was just masked. We made do with what we had, and hey, it wasn't that bad (at least not from my view).

Well, everything wasn't that bad except for the roof. I did my best over the first few years to tar, caulk, and have friends patch things here and there, all to no avail. Without a brand new roof, the amount of water coming in was too great, unstoppable, and causing more damage to accumulate over time. I was seriously afraid that the beams in the roof had rotted beyond repair and it wouldn't have surprised me to come in one day and find that the second floor had suddenly moved down to the first floor overnight. After awhile, I stopped replacing the tiles of the drop ceiling because it got too expensive. There was so much water up there that they'd come crashing down from the weight.

As a part of closing every night, we put at least twenty-five different buckets (and garbage cans) underneath certain ceiling tiles around the room. Above those specific ceiling tiles were homemade funnels of plastic sheeting that cascaded from the original metal ceiling above, which by the way was a disaster of rust and occasional falling pieces that had deteriorated due to the pouring in of rain. I had run that plastic sheeting all along the original upper ceiling to catch whatever water fell and collected it into one central bucket per area. If I hadn't done that, I surely would have needed 100 buckets. I even had one specific area that was so bad I had to use a 30-gallon trashcan when it rained.

The only problem was that the buckets and the 30-gallon trashcan soon began to overflow. There were times that we'd get to the karate school and the water on the severely warping hardwood floor would be a continuous puddle streaming from one end of the room to the other. It even got to the point where I found it necessary to poke a hole in the 30-gallon trashcan about one foot up from the bottom in order to run a drainage tube directly into the basement. This 30-gallon, homemade rain barrel, complete with funnels of plastic sheeting that was visible to the public, had become a permanent part of the karate school decor. It's a wonder that parents ever dropped their kids off to train in that eyesore of a place.

I won't even talk about the mold and mildew smell that place emitted. Sometimes, I'd enlist the student's help and we'd all get mops and brooms and proceed to sweep the water over to where the wall met the floor. There were certain places where the wall met the floorboards that provided a convenient drain down into the basement. This convenient drain actually consisted of large gaps that separated sections of the floor from the baseboard. Students also knew that they weren't to step on those specific areas of the floor because of the fear I had of them falling through. This nightmare went on for years until I could finally secure a loan to get the roof fixed.

I remember one day in particular, about six months before I got my loan, when the notion of *perspective* solidified in my brain. Class was about half over, in the rainforest (as we so affectionately called it), when it began to pour with rain outside. We scrambled and set out the buckets and then tried to continue with class. First, the pounding of the water was extremely distracting, and then all of the sudden, a loud disrupting clamor accompanied the descent of several of my ceiling tiles. The volume of water entering my 30-gallon can was more than even my drainage pipe could handle, and it didn't take long before it and all the other buckets were overflowing. Before the night was over, the water inside my training hall was ankle deep, and that's not an exaggeration.

By the time things started crashing down around us, I had already moved the students into the adjoining entrance where they would be safe and could wait for their parents. I thought for sure the roof would collapse that night. As you can imagine, a bunch of them were upset and thunderstruck at the calamity that was unfolding before their eyes. I needed to keep myself together as they were all looking at me to be their strength. It was there that I had the first of many talks to come about what I called "life lessons." The lesson for that day was "perspective." In the midst of all the chaos and fear of losing what was my dream, a school that I worked so hard to build, I calmly explained to the students that we will all have times in our lives when it seems as if everything around us is crashing down (sometimes literally). However, we must take a step back and focus on what's important.

Regardless of the stress I was feeling at the time, I was able to reach deep down inside and pull from within a great calming power (which I later would recognize as the Holy Spirit working in me). Sure, my building was in shambles, I was in fear of severe structural damage, and I thought for sure that I'd have to close down and give up the one thing that mattered most to me in life…teaching, but somehow I knew it would all be okay. It's not that I thought bad things wouldn't happen; it's just that I knew there was so much more to life. Everyone around me was safe. I could live for the moment and enjoy the presence of the wonderful people that were there for my support. I could also be thankful for the countless other things that I had in life, such as health, clothes on my back, and food to eat.

No matter how bad things got, I knew they could always be worse. Moreover, I was certain that there were many people out there in the world that had it much worse than I did. It was that day that I truly learned to let go of material possessions and place my efforts into building up the things that held true value in my life. I promised my students, and I also extend this same guarantee to you; if you learn to spotlight the positive things in your life, the negative things won't seem as significant. The negatives may not go away, but you'll recognize that they hold less value in your life. Soon your whole outlook will change. It's all about keeping things in perspective.

Since our world is only temporary (1 Corinthians 7:29-31[26]), we shouldn't be too wrapped up in it, either. Paul tells us to set our hearts on the things above, not on the things of this earth (Colossians 3:1-2[27]). In other words, our hearts should be on what is eternal, not on what is temporary. You see, things will come and go here on Earth. The flesh and blood we inhabit will pass away, but we can look forward to having a new and perfect body in Heaven. We are to inherit a kingdom where there will be no more pain and suffering. While temporary things on Earth need some attention, they probably don't need as much as we are accustomed to giving them. If we truly keep our life in perspective by focusing on the things above, then we'll catch a glimpse of our hope, which is in Heaven, and our temporary life won't seem as bad when rain gets in and our ceilings tumble down.

However, before we can focus on the things above, we must be able to see clearly. Our ancient ancestors thought that sight was a function of our eyes, sending out a signal or ray that bounced off objects and returned to create an image in our brain. Of course, we now know that sight is only possible because of light (outside of ourselves) that bounces off objects. Without an external source of light, we wouldn't be able to discern one thing from another because we'd constantly be in the dark. In life, Christ is our external light,

---

[26] 1 Corinthians 7:29-31 – What I mean, brothers, is that the time is short. From now on those who have wives should live as if they had none; those who mourn, as if they did not; those who are happy, as if they were not; those who buy something, as if it were not theirs to keep; those who use the things of the world, as if not engrossed in them. For this world in its present form is passing away.

[27] Colossians 3:1-2 – Since, then, you have been raised with Christ, set your hearts on things above, where Christ is seated at the right hand of God. Set your minds on things above, not on earthly things.

the Light of the World (John 8:12[28]), and the Light which guides our path (Psalm 119:105)[29]. Only with Him, can we see things clearly and thus focus on the things above.

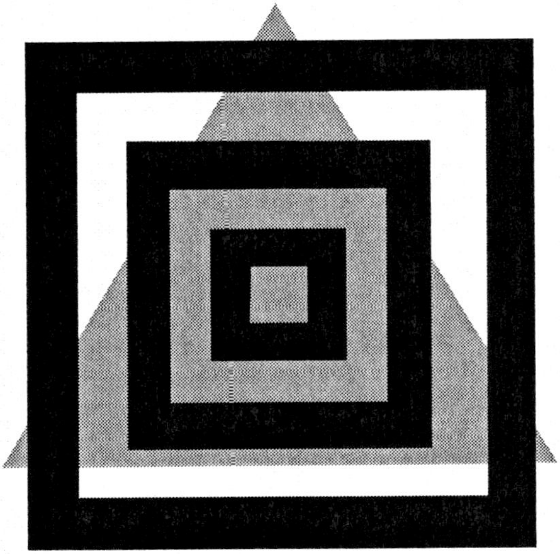

[28] John 8:12 – When Jesus spoke again to the people, He said, "I am the light of the world. Whoever follows me will never walk in darkness, but will have the light of life."

[29] Psalm 119:105 – Your word is a lamp to my feet and a light for my path.

12. The Secret to Learning

Life Lesson: We learn best what we teach.

One of the distinctions that set our studio apart from some other martial arts schools is the emphasis that we place on teaching students how to teach. Students learn how to work with beginners, give orientations, assist with classes, tutor other students, and even teach certain classes on their own. Certainly, there are times when it's useful for a busy instructor to have help and assistance in a classroom, and any good instructor wants to see others who can perpetuate the art. However, there's another reason why we teach students to teach, and I can assure you it's not for our own gain. Placing students in leadership roles is for the good of those students.

After all, there are risks that accompany this practice. Let's take for example the beginner orientations that mid-level students teach. This is the first impression that many people get when joining our school, and we leave it up to someone who is still in training. Are we crazy? No, we're just aware of the bigger picture and realize that we must have patience to allow our apprentice instructors to grow. By actively engaging students in the teaching experience, we inadvertently engage them in learning whatever it is that they are responsible for teaching.

Fact is we learn best what we teach. If you really want to learn something well, then just try teaching it. Suddenly, you're thrown into a completely new realm of knowing. Even if you think you know your stuff, you quickly learn that in order to teach it, you must know it about ten times better. For this reason, we encourage students to get all their senses involved in the learning process. The more senses involved, the greater chance they will retain the information being taught. Consider a research study done by National Training Laboratories in Bethel, Maine. Students retain only 5% if the information is presented solely in a lecture format. However, they retain 10% if actively involved in reading; 20% if audio/visual aids are used; 30% from demonstrations; 50% from discussion groups; 75% from active participation, and 90% when engaged in teaching others the material. When learning their martial arts techniques, our students say the name of the technique to incorporate cognitive recall, speech, and hearing. When demonstrating the technique, they focus on form, speed, and/or power to incorporate sight and feeling.

Good teachers rarely teach material the same way twice. This is because every student has individual needs and different learning styles. Even though students may hold the same rank, they learn very differently. Learning is heightened when instructors adjust their teaching methods to the learning styles of their students. It is maximized when instructors also understand what their students are capable of doing with the material that is being taught. Because instructors are required to know the material from so many different physical, mental, and spiritual angles (in order to teach it to so many different kinds of students) they are forced to learn from perspectives and styles that extend far beyond their own. This learning process develops a new and improved understanding of the martial arts and promotes proficiency at all levels.

The tool that we use to determine what students are physically, mentally, and spiritually capable of doing with various kinds of martial arts material is the *learning ladder*, a figurative ladder with four rungs. At the top of the ladder (fourth rung) is the ultimate level of proficiency. We always begin at the bottom of the ladder in everything we do, but our goal is to move towards the top. The first rung is for the *unconsciously unskilled.* This is where someone does not know how to do or is completely unaware of something. The phrase "ignorance is bliss" could very well describe this rung. If or when a person suddenly becomes aware of this missing link, then he/she moves to the next rung on the ladder.

The second rung is for the *consciously unskilled.* It takes very little to move to this rung. On this rung, someone is lacking and knows it. This is where I find myself with most things! Although, I guess if I were on the first rung with most things, I would still believe in my own mind that I was on the second rung because I wouldn't be aware of the difference. Think about it. It's moving to the next rung on the learning ladder that separates the boys from the men and is truly the toughest transition of all four rungs. It takes practice and a great deal of patience to climb to the next level.

The third rung is for the *consciously skilled.* This is where you become proficient at an activity, but you have to concentrate very hard in order to carry it out. Don't be too discouraged if you're hanging around on this rung for a considerable amount of time. It takes practice, practice, and more practice before you can even think about the fourth rung, which is for the *unconsciously skilled.* This rung is the ultimate goal for things that we want to learn and do. On the forth rung, one can process information subconsciously and react to situations instantaneously. It's allowing your mind to go along on cruise control of whatever it is you are unconsciously skilled at doing.

Driving is an example of what we can cultivate on the forth rung, some better than others. Another example is the unique ability that musicians possess. If you talk to good musicians, they'll tell you that they don't consciously think about the sheet music and playing the instrument. After awhile their brains automatically process the music and skip the part of consciously identifying a C sharp and how a note is obtained from the instrument. This takes an incredible amount of perseverance and determination. Don't give up. As someone once said, "The race is not always to the swift, but to those who keep on running."

My French teacher said that you can tell when you really know a foreign language because you begin to think and/or dream in it. Now that's rung four. I guess, depending on what you're trying to learn, it can take a lot of time. Just think back to your ABCs in first grade. Are you reading this book now, seeing the word "learn," and saying to yourself, "L – E – A – R – N" as you struggle with the phonetics and decide what to do with the "A?" No, you probably just read the word "learn" all at once in the previous sentence without even giving it a second thought. Congratulations, your reading skill is on the forth rung.

Now, we don't do all this climbing on our own. The ladder belongs to God, but it's His strength (given to us by the Holy Spirit) that enables us to grasp the rungs and move up. Spiritually speaking, we are born on the first rung and haven't a clue about God. Next, we move to the second rung when we come to understand that there is a God and that we have much to learn about Him. He continues to help us move up on the ladder in learning how to follow Him until we begin to do so unconsciously. Soon, we are walking on the straight and narrow path (Matthew 7:13-14)[30] and on our way to experiencing the true joy that God desires for us.

When apprentice teachers understand the material that they are teaching and they understand how to use the learning ladder to determine what students are capable of doing and how to teach them, they unconsciously become masters at learning. It is often through teaching that one can truly master the material that he/she has learned, because it is only through teaching that one can see how the material fits people from a variety of different perspectives. When you were a student, you learned how to do a front snap kick one way, but as a teacher, you will learn how to do a front snap kick 10 or more different ways, and your technique will dramatically improve. This is why the secret to learning is to teach.

---

[30] Matthew 7:13-14 – Enter through the narrow gate. For wide is the gate and broad is the road that leads to destruction, and many enter through it. But small is the gate and narrow the road that leads to life, and only a few find it.

13. Set Your Eyes on the Prize

Life Lesson: For <u>with</u> God all things are possible. ~ Mark 10:27[31]

In ancient times, there was no such thing as colored belts that symbolized rank. Belts were only viewed in a practical sense, such as to hold up people's pants or keep their tops in place. After years of blood, sweat, dirt, and grime that came from training in the martial arts, these light colored *practical* belts naturally turned black. People weren't awarded black belts; they acquired them through years of training. In other words, if someone's belt was dark, and bloodstained (black), it was obvious that he had been training for a long time.

Whoever came up with the idea to award a full color belt system based on this natural process was a true genius who must have understood the value of setting goals. Unlike before, degrees of proficiency could now be marked through tangible short-term goals, and earning a black belt could be planned for the first time. Now, the black belt degree didn't seem so distant. Students could see the accomplishments they were making along the way, and focus on a long-term goal through a series of steps in the short-term.

People of all ages benefit from goal setting, but setting goals is especially crucial to the development of young people. I remember being a white belt as a young boy and taking my first test in the martial arts. I was going for my yellow belt and didn't really know what to expect. Of course, there were the anticipated challenges of a grueling physical test, but what really threw me was the written exam. Apart from the book knowledge that I was supposed to know, there was an essay question that helped to significantly influence my upcoming success in the martial arts: "How far do you want to go in karate?"

---

[31] <u>Mark 10:27</u> – Jesus looked at them and said, "With man this is impossible, but not with God; all things are possible with God."

Frankly, I hadn't thought much about it. Since I didn't really know how far I wanted to go, my answer simply reflected what I thought the instructor wanted to hear. I wrote that I wanted to earn my black belt and someday teach others. What I didn't write was that I had no confidence in myself and, didn't think I could achieve that level. Because of this question, I found myself spending a lot of time pondering exactly what it was that I wanted to do with the martial arts. Was I just interested in learning the bare minimum to be able to defend myself and then quit? I knew I wanted to get better, but when would the *better* turn into *good enough*?

I knew part of the reason I was there was to exercise and lose weight, but even then, I had no tangible goals. How much weight did I want to lose? When would it be enough? It's like getting into a car, and driving without knowing where you're going. After all, the reason why we get into cars is usually to go to a destination. If you don't know where you are going, you could be wasting precious time and resources; or worse yet, you could be heading in the opposite direction of what you someday might choose as a destination. Without careful planning and a clear destination (or tangible goals), you are probably just spinning your wheels.

Once I determined that I indeed wanted to become a black belt and help others the way that I had been helped, my approach to training changed tremendously. Once I knew where I was going, I could make decisions about my current situations and how they would ultimately affect my long-term goals. It took many years of hard training, but I eventually received my black belt. In fact, along the way I ended up setting additional goals for myself, some of which I've far exceeded and others to this day have yet to come to fruition. Nevertheless, I'll still keep on truckin' and never give up.

No matter what it is that we want to accomplish in life, we need to set goals or targets. Imagine someone who calls himself an archer but doesn't have a goal or target for his bow and arrows. Without a target, the archer has no purpose and nothing by which to measure his success. In fact, he isn't really an archer at all; he's just a funny guy who likes to shoot arrows in the air. Before investing our time, energy, and resources in anything, we should have clear goals.

When identifying a long-term goal, don't expect to get there with great ease. You must be willing to persevere and be patient, to set and reach a series of short-term goals before expecting to see the long-term ones. John F. Kennedy once said, "All this will not be finished in the first one hundred days. Nor will it be finished in the first thousand days, nor in the life of this administration, nor even perhaps in our lifetime on this planet. But let us begin." Push yourself to reach new heights. If you accomplish them with little or no effort, then aim higher and higher until it's a challenge.

Long-term goals should be measurable and realistic. You wouldn't want to say that your goal is to be happy. Such a goal is realistic, but subjective and can't be measured. A measurable goal might be to get married and have a baby because you obviously know when you've accomplished it. In a similar manner, a goal of getting married and having children with the richest woman in the world is indeed possible, but not very realistic. A realistic goal would be to marry a beautiful woman that has similar values to you and who sees herself as a daughter of God.

Short-term goals must carry the same attributes; just on a smaller scale. These goals are necessary to mark a person's progress and to provide little stepping-stones along the path to the larger goal. Keep in mind, a journey of a thousand miles begins with only one step. Therefore, don't concentrate too hard on the long-term goal, but be positive and focus your attention on accomplishing the short-term ones. If you only have your eye on the final destination, then you are not taking occasional breaks to notice the progress you've made along the way.

Take a moment (just a moment) from time to time to look down and look back to see the progress you've made.

Taking time to evaluate your situation can help you make decisions about what is necessary to move forward. Also, the self-confidence that can be reaped from celebrating your goals can be tremendously helpful. Just remember, there are more mountains to climb to get where you want to go. It's important to simultaneously know where you're going (your long-term goal), how to get there (your short-term goals), and where you're at in relationship to those goals (marking your progress along the way).

Look at the book of Ezra. The temple in Jerusalem had been destroyed by Nebuchadnezzar, the King of Babylon, when he exiled the people from their land. It wasn't until some time later that Cyrus, King of Persia, led by God, gave the order to allow the Israelites to return and rebuild the temple (Ezra 1:2[32]). Talking about a seemingly impossible task, this was a long-term goal! To rebuild the temple was a tremendous undertaking in that day and age. Although they knew it would take decades to complete, they went forward anyway. They made a plan, set smaller goals, and remained committed to their task. You can even read about all the types of opposition they encountered along the way, but they still kept their eyes on their goal and never gave up.

How were they able to continue this project to the end? In Matthew 19[33], we learn that "with God, all things are possible." They would never have been able to complete it on their own. I've also been in many situations in my life where I couldn't have made it on my own. It has only been through

---

[32] Ezra 2:1 – This is what Cyrus king of Persia says: The LORD, the God of heaven, has given me all the kingdoms of the earth and he has appointed me to build a temple for him at Jerusalem in Judah.

[33] Matthew 19:24-26 – Again I tell you, it is easier for a camel to go through the eye of a needle than for a rich man to enter the kingdom of God." When the disciples heard this, they were greatly astonished and asked, "Who then can be saved?" Jesus looked at them and said, "With man this is impossible, but with God all things are possible."

the strength and power that I've received from the Lord that I've been able to persevere through occasions that otherwise looked bleak. John definitely knew what he was talking about when he wrote that he wasn't able to do anything on his own (John 5:30a[34]). Only with God can you achieve much. Just lean on His power and allow Him to carry you!

[34] John 5:30 – By myself I can do nothing.

14. Attitudes are Contagious

Life Lesson: A positive attitude is not only good for you, but for everyone else that you encounter.

Henry Ford once said, "Whether you think you can, or whether you think you can't, you're right." Along these lines, there's an amazing bunch of fortunetellers in my school. These students have a near perfect success rate in predicting their own future, and some success in shaping the future of others around them. Are they clairvoyant? Of course not. Have they received some special revelation from God that the rest of us have not? No. The secret to their fortune telling ability is their state of mind and attitude towards the present. Regardless of their natural abilities, students that come to class with a positive attitude achieve great things. They jump over hurdles, they plow through roadblocks, and nothing stops them from ultimately reaching the other side. This is how ordinary people become champions.

One person's attitude can affect many. My mother once taught me this lesson as a kid when we found some rotten apples in the refrigerator. When one rotten apple touches any number of other apples, the other apples become rotten, too. The same truth applies with people and the attitudes they display in life. Like it or not, we're all massed together in an apple bin called Earth. We come into contact with hundreds of people every day, which affect each and every one of their lives in some way, shape, or form. If we're moldy and rotten, then we probably infect other people with our negativity. However, if we're positive and pure, then we can help to inspire and motivate them. A positive attitude can cheer folks up and instill an *I CAN* (versus an *I Can't*) sentiment.

I've seen situations in karate school, and maybe you have, too, where positive attitudes spread like wild fire. When a student walks into class and is excited about learning, a piece of that excitement rubs off on others and the whole class does very well. Just one spark from a positive individual can ignite a fire in a large group that will keep burning. On the other hand, negativity can have the same kind of impact. Unfortunately, it can sometimes take very little to douse the positive fires in people. I have seen several fine organizations destroyed by gossip, lack of enthusiasm, jealously, and discord. You may not think you have that much influence on the world around you, but like it or not... you do!

Do people have positive attitudes because they have perfect lives? Absolutely not! You can read the Psalms to see perfect examples of this fact. You can also look at the many people around you who have severe troubles in their lives, but choose not to wallow in their pain. These people find things to smile about every day. Consider the following strategies:

- "A person is as happy as he makes up his mind to be." (Abraham Lincoln)
- "I, not events have the power to make me happy or unhappy today. I can choose which it shall be. Yesterday is dead, tomorrow hasn't arrived yet. I have just one day, today, and I'm going to be happy in it." (Groucho Marx)
- Everything can be taken from a man but one thing: the last of the human freedoms, to choose one's attitude in any given set of circumstances, to choose one's own way." (Victor Frankl)

Although I agree wholeheartedly with these strategies, I will caution you to be careful when putting on your happy face. The trick is to balance your positive attitude with reality. I don't recommend putting on a false front and pretending that everything is grand. Denial can dangerously disconnect you from reality. Sometimes it's good to let folks know that not everything is alright. People appreciate it when you let down your walls and allow them to know that you're a "real" person who has struggles, too.

There's a difference between being real and being negative. At one of my former jobs, I used to know a produce deliveryman who came into our store to deliver food about twice a week. Among the employees, he was commonly known as *Desolate Dan*. First, he was always late, and second he complained regularly about how everything in his life stunk! At first, we sympathized with him and did our best to listen to ALL of his problems. However, somewhere in the second month, we began to dread his arrival. Looking back, I realize that Dan was truly in need and I should have been more responsive to his pain. So many individuals in our world see nothing but the dark side of life. Our goal should be to live realistically, and not to be caught up in the gloomy world of pessimists or the skewed world of those who see absolutely everything through rose-colored glasses.

We have a God-given ability to choose a positive attitude. In other words, we can make a decision to be a thermostat instead of a mere thermometer. A thermostat controls the temperature in its environment; however, a thermometer simply reflects the temperature around it. Is your mood dictated by the circumstances in your life? Does your environment control your reading? Alternatively, are you more like the thermostat? Do you set the tone for the world in which you live? Are you in control of your feelings and emotions? Do you have the power to choose to be happy no matter what the circumstance? Will you, according to your attitude, positively influence others who are thermometers, and cause them to rise?

As Christians, we take this truth one step further. It's not just that we have the unique ability to recognize the good things and be thankful for the blessings in our lives; it's that we're focused on the big picture. We know that we are loved by God and have an assurance that we'll be with Him forever in Heaven. We know that what happens here on Earth is just temporary and what matters most is the relationship we have with our Lord and Savior, Jesus Christ, who offers us all of what we truly need. When people see this positive attitude reflected in our persevering and maybe even see us smiling through rough circumstances, they desire to know more. In 1 Peter 3:15[35], we learn that we should always be ready to give an answer to everyone who asks about the hope in us.

We never know when others may be watching us. We never know when our attitudes may spread like a blazing fire. We never know when our lives may or can be a testimony that drastically transforms the life of another. Therefore, I encourage you to live your life as if every moment were critical. Live life in the present and make the most of every opportunity you have. Make the decision to be happy and bask in the glory of God's radiance. Enjoy the blessings that you've been given and focus on the positive aspects of life. No matter what our circumstances, we all have much to be thankful for and we can accomplish so much more with the right attitude.

[35] 1 Peter 3:15 – But in your hearts set apart Christ as Lord. Always be prepared to give an answer to everyone who asks you to give the reason for the hope that you have. But do this with gentleness and respect.

15. Losing has Purpose

Life Lesson: Only by losing can you learn how to win.

I remember competing in my first tournament as a young boy just as if it were yesterday. I had been preparing for this competition for quite some time. My technique was polished (or at least I thought so), and I was emotionally pumped and determined to bring home a trophy. Although I didn't know it at the time, I now realize that it was just my low self-esteem that was seeking a pat on the back from my family, my instr-ucttors, and most of all me. Anyway, I can truly say that I gave it my best shot, but I didn't win.

My heart sank into my chest when the judges called out the last winner, and I was left standing as a loser. I had failed. What would my family and instructors think of me? Would they think I wasn't any good? I felt awful and didn't know what to do but cry. I cried even harder when people I knew were around. I wasn't consciously faking it; my tears were for real. Maybe I was just looking for that attention or comfort that I didn't get by winning the trophy that day. My self-esteem was on empty and it needed to be filled at once.

What I really needed to learn was how to lose, but first I had to learn that my self-worth wasn't supposed to come from beating others in tournaments. After all, if I had won, someone else would have lost and this would have made my self-worth contingent on other people losing. I didn't understand that I was a winner just for going out there and giving it my best, and little did I know that losing would end up teaching me so much more about life.

While success is the ultimate goal for most of us, failure is important, too. Consider all you have to learn from losing a tournament. Think about the thrill of the game when the outcome is uncertain and recognize the character and strength that comes out of being bested by another. Losing is painful, but like a vaccination, it prepares you for much stronger setbacks in life. Life's journey is full of ups and downs. Learn to celebrate the *ups* and not think your world is ending when you experience a *down*. If you've prepared and given your best, and maintained a good attitude along the way, then failure can be a positive thing in your life. Sure, not everything worked out the way you wanted, but there's always next time. You've lived to fight another day.

As Christians, we must personally understand failure if we are to ever find success. If we read the Old Testament, we see that God set some immense hurdles in front of us. Actually, they're much more than hurdles. In fact, God's Law (the Ten Commandments) is more like jumping over Mount Everest. Imagine God the Father in Heaven (or in the clouds of Everest) asking us to jump up to Him. Nobody can do it! Some might be able to jump two feet in the air and others may be able to jump six, but in the end, it really doesn't matter because none of us even come close to reaching Him. We lose no matter how high we've jumped.

When it comes to God, the stakes for losing aren't just that of a trivial game or contest. No, these stakes are life and death. If we lose, we're out of the game for good... for eternity. In Luke 10:25-28[36] Jesus Himself stated that the way for man (and He means woman too) to get into Heaven is to "Love the Lord your God with all your heart and with all your soul and with all your strength and with your entire mind." If that wasn't impossible enough, Jesus threw on one more weight by adding, "And, love your neighbor as yourself!"

---

[36] Luke 10:25-28 – On one occasion an expert in the law stood up to test Jesus. "Teacher," he asked, "what must I do to inherit eternal life?" "What is written in the Law?" He replied. "How do you read it?" He answered: "'Love the Lord your God with all your heart and with all your soul and with all your strength and with all your mind'; and, 'Love your neighbor as yourself.'" "You have answered correctly," Jesus replied. "Do this and you will live."

Wow! Talk about impossible. The great Mother Teresa herself couldn't even live up to those standards.

Fortunately, God doesn't judge us by our efforts or accomplishments. At the end of our life on Earth, He doesn't decide whether we'll spend eternity with Him based on how well we've kept His law and commandments. He provides for us another option since He knows that we can't live up to the Law. There's only one that could ever keep the law perfectly, and that's Jesus! In Ephesians 2:8[37], the Bible promises eternal life with Christ to those who have faith in Jesus. Yes! There is hope after all, at least for those who don't refuse Him.

Through Jesus Christ, and because of Him, we can be confident of joining God in Heaven someday. However, there are benefits for us while we live here on Earth, too. For all of us losers, we can hold our head up high knowing that our self-worth isn't based on whether or not we live up to God's standards. Rather, it is derived from knowing that God loves us and has a special plan for our lives. We can realize our worth and have self-confidence that we are here to serve Him and live as His own because we are loved by Him in a way that spans beyond human comprehension. Nobody can ever take that away from us, so rejoice! Tournaments come and go, but God is forever.

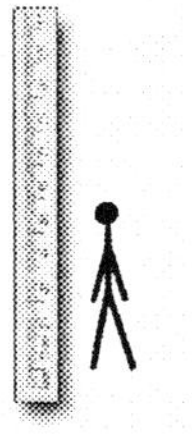

[37] Ephesians 2:8 – For it is by grace you have been saved, through faith– and this not from yourselves, it is the gift of God.

16. When Tension Mounts

Life Lesson: An ounce of resolution can cure a pound of conflict.

The environment in which I studied karate was very militant, strict, and regimented. The hard-nosed master gave orders and everyone jumped at his commands, no questions asked. In a way, our fear of the master was actually positive. It motivated us to push ourselves to extremes and give 110% to our training. Furthermore, it taught us to be disciplined, focused, and self-reliant. To this day, I still hold much respect and gratitude for my instructor and how much he taught me. He provided me with a great foundation upon which I've continued to grow and build my life.

Nonetheless, there was also a negative side to this militant environment. While we were well trained in dealing with physical conflict, we were not conditioned in emotional or mental conflict resolution. I regret the many interpersonal struggles within the group, and that none of us knew how to handle them. Admittedly, I share blame in contributing to these struggles because all I did about them was complain behind people's backs. I was a teenager at the time and didn't understand the first thing about effective conflict resolution. Instead of complaining to others, I should have brought my issues directly to the people involved.

Since then, I have learned some very positive and effective ways of resolving conflict. First, don't jump to conclusions without knowing the facts. In other words, if a friend walks by without so much as an acknowledgement, you shouldn't assume that he is ignoring you. Sure, he could have been intentionally trying to snub you, or he could have not recognized or noticed you because he was daydreaming or wasn't paying attention. Whatever the reason, the smartest thing to do is to give the other person the benefit of the doubt until you have a chance to discuss it and find out the truth.

Second, try to resolve conflict personably and quickly. I always recommend a good old face-to-face chat as opposed to an email or letter. Express your concern in a polite and respectful manner. Then, give the person an opportunity to offer an explanation. While this method won't always result in a solution, it will at least provide you with firsthand, information as to where the other person stands. Remember that understanding each other's point of views doesn't mean that you both agree with each other. If you do not agree, but you at least understand each other, then you have still made significant progress. Depending on the situation, you may just need to bring in a third party that you both can trust.

There are people that would disagree with me about raising points of contention with someone else. Some feel that Christians should avoid interpersonal conflict at all cost. Now, if the offense is something silly and minor, then go ahead and let it go. After all, we can't be nit-picky about every little thing. However, there's nothing wrong with setting up some boundaries to protect yourself (and others). Don't misuse Matthew 5:39[38], and also take care not to go way off the other end by sacrificing personal relationships because you think that everything has to be your way.

This brings me to the third way that you can positively and effectively resolve conflict; set clear boundaries in your life without imposing your way on others. It is important to find balance on the fine line between being a pushover and pushing people over. When we allow others to cross our boundaries and take advantage of us, we are enabling and encouraging them to continue in the negative behavior. We don't have their best interest in mind and we certainly don't have the best interest of others in mind, since chances are the behavior isn't limited to us.

Sometimes people need tough love, and sometimes we just need to speak up in order to help the people grow. What

---

[38] Matthew 5:39 – But I tell you, Do not resist an evil person. If someone strikes you on the right cheek, turn to him the other also.

kind of a friend would I be if I allowed my buddy to walk around all day with a booger dangling from the end of his nose without his knowledge? As awkward as it may be for some of us to confront our friends with embarrassing issues, we're really doing them a favor in the long term by drawing their attention to the matter. The same is true with difficult interpersonal relationship issues. Looking at the big picture, it's best if we talk to others about the major issues of concern we have with their lives or behaviors.

Let's look at Matthew 18:15-16[39], where Jesus teaches on the concept of conflict resolution. First, He instructs us to handle these matters privately. Keep in mind that He is talking about *personal* matters and there are exceptions to this rule. If you're physically violated (i.e. robbed or assaulted), then it's not a personal matter and you should get help. Second, Jesus instructs us to go back and take one or two others if a private meeting doesn't work. Note, He doesn't tell us to make assumptions and gossip behind other people's backs. He also doesn't tell us to ignore the problem and not do anything about it.

Try to remember that conflict isn't bad. In fact, plenty of good can come out of a struggle with someone else. In many cases, people will actually become closer friends if they can work through controversy with one another; that is, if the controversy is handled in a mature and productive manner. Conflict can build strength and character. Think of working on your conflict resolution techniques as weight lifting for your mind; resistance is necessary for growth. Why do you suppose educational institutions spend so much money to

---

[39] Matthew 18:15-16 – If your brother sins against you, go and show him his fault, just between the two of you. If he listens to you, you have won your brother over. But if he will not listen, take one or two others along, so that every matter may be established by the testimony of two or three witnesses.

sponsor debate teams? They realize the value of both competition and civilized conflict.

A friend once told me a story that helps us understand the value of conflict-resolution. Once upon a time, God told a man to go out and push on a huge boulder for thirty minutes every day. So, every day the man went out and pushed. He pushed day after day, week after week, and even month after month. After some time had passed, the devil appeared to the man. "You've been pushing on this boulder for months," the devil said. "All this time and you've gone nowhere. You're making no progress. Isn't God unfair for giving you a task that He knows you can't complete?" The man became very discouraged and prayed to God, "Lord, I can't move this boulder. Why have you told me to do so when you know it's beyond my ability?" God answered the man, "I never told you to move the boulder; I just told you to push because I wanted you to get stronger. From pushing on the boulder all this time, your legs, back, and arms are all very powerful. Now you are ready to tackle my plan because you have the might to accomplish it."

In this story, the man could have assumed that God didn't care about him because of what the devil said, but he had the wisdom to ask God about it and in doing so, the conflict was resolved. Often times, conflict is nothing more than a misunderstanding or a misinterpretation of words, thoughts, or behaviors. While God had good intentions and pushing the boulder turned out to be a good thing for the man, it could have been a disaster had the conflict between God and the man not been dealt with appropriately. The man could have strayed from the will of God and not done the work that God was preparing him to do. So, the next time to you think you may jump to conclusions, make sure know where you're jumping before you spring in the air and land.

17. What Goes In, Must Come Out

Life Lesson: The mind is like a fertile garden, it will grow anything you wish to plant.
~ Bruce Lee

A few belts before achieving my black belt, a small group of us students were beginning to push our bodies beyond our comfort zones and explore the actual limits of what we could do. We decided it would be both fun and challenging to see if we could incorporate some gymnastics into our art. For me, physical training was always difficult. I'm not the most athletic person and wasn't born with much raw talent, but I think this added challenge helped me to stay motivated. We worked on tumbling, cartwheels, front flips, and front handsprings. It took a lot of effort, but it was precisely this sort of challenge that kept us interested.

After months of effort, we were ready to incorporate some of these acrobatic maneuvers into the choreography of our demonstrations. I felt good about our accomplishments, but there was one major obstacle in the way of my being completely satisfied. I had an intense fear of doing a back flip and I wasn't about to give up until I had conquered it. What terrified me the most was that I couldn't see where I was going. Every time I tried to go over backwards, I would inevitably twist my body and look over one of my shoulders. I was chicken! No matter how much I trained my body, I wasn't getting anywhere because my mind remained weak.

Since fear is a product of the mind, it can usually be controlled. Too often we *imagine* how bad a situation could be, and don't allow it to simply be what it is. Bruce Lee once said, "The mind is like a fertile garden, it will grow anything you wish to plant." Like water helps a garden to grow, visualization and meditation helped me overcome my fear of the back flip and improve my technique. Visualization is when we purposely and consciously direct a vision into the subconscious mind. Meditation is when we direct a thought, idea, or concept into the subconscious mind through a highly contemplative state of focus. In addition, meditation is usually accompanied by some relaxation techniques that free up hindrances from the body to better focus.

I recommend visualization and meditation techniques to anyone who is having trouble accomplishing a certain goal. These techniques help us to direct the subconscious mind, which is always on and functioning. Have you ever forgotten to blink or to breathe? Of course not, because your autopilot (or subconscious mind) is always on. Not only is it always on, but it is also trainable. It helps us to walk and talk at the same time, steer a car at 75 MPH while daydreaming, respond with martial arts techniques when attacked, go through our forms, and much more.

When I was meditating in my early years, I learned to use of the power of visualization. I would imagine myself accomplishing whatever goal I desired. Note this isn't just a quick thought, but a purposeful and long process in which you repeatedly lose yourself in a vision that represents the accomplishing of your goal. For best results, repeat the vision until some of your senses almost seem real. Imagine the smells, the sounds, the feeling, and what it looks like for you to be accomplishing your goal. If you clearly and vividly imagine yourself doing, being, and having the things and qualities you truly want, then you are using positive imagery or visualization to accomplish your goals.

Do you have any fears that you would like to conquer and overcome? As you meditate and visualize, confront these fears and obstacles. Become familiar with them and imagine that they are growing smaller and smaller. The subconscious mind is incredible and you'll begin to notice a difference after some regular sessions. While it may not be your only method of accomplishing a particular goal, these tools certainly can be very effective. The Bible teaches on visualization and meditation. Philippians 4:8 reads, "Finally, brothers, whatever is true, whatever is noble, whatever is right, whatever is pure, whatever is lovely, whatever is admirable--if anything is excellent or praiseworthy - think about such things."

Because visualization and meditation are powerful techniques that can work for or against you, you should use them wisely and only within the boundaries set forth in the Word of God. Using these techniques for selfish gain or evil purposes is spiritual suicide. In others words, do not visualize or meditate on anything that is not true, noble, right, pure, lovely, admirable, excellent, or praiseworthy. The apostle Paul was a wise man. He knew that what goes in must come out. If we fill ourselves with filth, then filth will come out. However, if we fill ourselves with good and positive things, then good and positive things will come out. It's no different from eating. If we fill ourselves with junk, our bodies will be sluggish. If we eat right, then our bodies will be strong.

In addition to consciously directing what you meditate on and visualize, you should control the people with whom you associate and the environments to which you subject yourself. Doing so will help prevent negative messages from infecting your subconscious mind in the same way that washing your hands helps prevent germs from invading your body. Paul knew that these things play a vital role in the way we think and act (Philippians 4:8)[40]. Furthermore, a man is known by the company he keeps. People associate you with your friends. You are also influenced by the people around you. If your friends or associates are gloomy and pessimistic, chances are that you will be perceived and will feel this way, too.

I once worked in a restaurant and was very surprised at the level of profanity, sexually-oriented conversations, and negativity that occurred in the kitchen. I kept praying that in some small way I'd be a positive influence; however, in spite

[40] Philippians 4:8 – Finally, brothers, whatever is true, whatever is noble, whatever is right, whatever is pure, whatever is lovely, whatever is admirable–if anything is excellent or praiseworthy–think about such things.

of my strong Christian convictions, I caught myself thinking some of those kitchen thoughts from time to time. Believe me; I know how people can be easily influenced by their environment. I thank the Lord every day for the gamut of Christian brothers and sisters I have around me now. I need them in my life to keep me focused and on track.

On a positive note, I've begun listening to so much Christian music over the last number of years that the tunes are seemingly stuck in my head for good; I can't stop them from playing repeatedly in my mind. If music has this kind of influence on a person, then isn't it even more important to choose carefully what sort of lyrics and messages we allow to enter our brains? I've also seen hypnotists do some very scary things to folks. Of course, they were all harmless antics as a part of a variety show, but the scary part was the realization of the power that the mind can wield.

I often put on a soft background CD at night when I go to bed. Sometimes I play positive music, and sometimes I play soundtracks with optimistic messages. A recording of scripture or even a tape full of information you're trying to learn for a test can do wonders. Remember that the mind is always at work. Even when the conscious may be sleeping, the subconscious is putting in overtime. From my own experience, I can attest that visualization, meditation, and subliminal messaging do make a world of difference. The mind is a powerful thing, and we haven't even begun to unlock its potential.

18. Thank You!

Life Lesson: There's nothing more beautiful in life than the presence and joy of a thankful optimist.

In my many years of instructing martial arts, I've had the pleasure of working with a number of students with both physical and mental challenges. I've had students with missing appendages, ADD, Tourette's syndrome, asthma; I have worked with folks who were confined to wheelchairs, and even an individual who was blind. In every case, I have walked away learning (and re-learning) two very important lessons. First, the will or spirit can overcome a multitude of challenges. Second, it's important to be thankful for the blessings and gifts that we have in life, and to focus our attention on what's truly important.

When people are motivated and determined to succeed, little can stand in their way. A few years ago, a student of mine was in a motorcycle accident and suffered both physically and mentally from severe brain trauma. This individual has since overcome incredible odds and has made outstanding strides in his recovery. It's not because his road to recovery was smooth; believe me, it's a rough and rocky road and he has many miles yet to travel. It's because he fights tooth and nail for every ounce of recovery. His determination and willpower is remarkable. Whenever I consider an obstacle too great, I think about him and his success as my inspiration.

Another incredible inspiration in my life is my mother. I owe so much to her and all the things she's taught me in life. More than anything, she taught me about staying positive and making the most of what I have. The last third of her life was filled with the torture of living with an uncommon disease called sclera-derma. Mom was burdened with this disease for about 20 years, in which she endured an enormous amount of suffering. It started out by slowly affecting her digestive system. Throughout the years, she endured incredible pain in her back and her extremities. She lost fingers and toes, underwent several operations, and eventually lost her ability to eat anything at all. Her last several years on this Earth were spent hooked up to a feeding tube every night and receiving her daily nutrients intravenously. In the end, she bled to death internally and there was nothing that the doctors could do to prevent it.

I feel badly that I can't justly describe or convey the anguish my mother went through. What I can say is that she was always optimistic. I never heard her complain and cry, "Why me?" I never heard her focusing on herself and the pain she was suffering. She was notorious for enjoying the things that she could do in life. I watched her play golf when she could barely even grip the clubs due to the throbbing pain in her hands. I watched her put on countless smiling faces when the grandkids would come over to play. She was very active with her family and friends and always enjoyed their company. In addition, right up to the end, she was a regular at the bingo hall. Mom was incredible. I hate to admit that if I had been in her shoes, I would have been complaining and feeling sorry for myself the whole time.

Yes, my mom was a real trooper, a black belt grand master at heart. Every new and debilitating challenge just made her more aware of how lucky she was for the wonderful things in life that she had. Her focus was on the positive and the things that were in her favor. She amazed us all (doctors especially) that she survived as long as she did. Twenty years with this disease was much more than anyone ever expected. I'm convinced it was a combination of her positive attitude, thankful spirit, and the love she had for her family that kept her going. I'm grateful to you mom for setting such a wonderful example and teaching us all the value of staying positive and being thankful for the blessings in our lives! Thank you!

I now try my best to begin each day with the attitude of making the most of what I have. When I work out, I'm thankful that I can walk. When I read, I'm thankful for my intellectual abilities and for my sight. When I wake up, I'm thankful that I'm healthy. When I eat, I'm thankful that I can afford more than the bare minimum to sustain my life. When it rains, I thank God for providing me shelter and a warm bed. It's amazing how much your outlook on life changes when you take time to be thankful for what you have and realize that there are so many more individuals out there that would give anything to be in your shoes. No matter where you are in life, always consider those less fortunate than you. You may think that nobody else in the world has it rougher than you have it, but believe me, there are plenty of people that do.

Some of my favorite Bible passages on thankfulness include Ephesians 5:20[41], Colossians 3:15[42], 1 Thessalonians 5:18[43], Deuteronomy 12:7[44], Psalm 35:9[45], Psalm 118:24[46], Philippians 4:4[47]. I don't know about you, but all this giving

---

[41] Ephesians 5:20 – Always give thanks to God the Father for everything, in the name of our Lord Jesus Christ.

[42] Colossians 3:15 – Let the peace of Christ rule in your hearts, since as members of one body you were called to peace. And be thankful.

[43] 1 Thessalonians 5:18 – Give thanks in all circumstances, for this is God's will for you in Christ Jesus.

[44] Deuteronomy 12:7 – There, in the presence of the LORD your God, you and your families shall eat and shall rejoice in everything you have put your hand to, because the LORD your God has blessed you.

[45] Psalm 35:9 – Then my soul will rejoice in the LORD and delight in His salvation.

[46] Psalm 118:24 – This is the day the LORD has made; let us rejoice and be glad in it.

[47] Philippians 4:4 – Rejoice in the Lord always. I will say it again: Rejoice!

thanks and rejoicing inspires me. I feel compelled to share what I have with those around me. I want to go out and spread the good news about God, and how He has changed my life. I guess that's one of the reasons I'm writing this book. My joy doesn't just compel me to talk, but it inspires me to do good. Because of the incomprehensible grace and forgiveness that I've received through Christ's love, I want to spread grace and forgiveness throughout the world by way of my actions.

You see, we no longer live under the Law of things we *have to do* from the Old Testament. Giving to others and doing good deeds are not payments to obtain our rescue. When Jesus came, He fulfilled the Law by paying for our sins and debts. We no longer *have* to…we *want* to! It's for this precise reason that I can't help but to give and do for others in my life. It makes me happy to give to the Church and know that I'm privileged to participate in some small way in the work that the Lord wishes to be carried out here on Earth. Therefore, I give my time, talent, and treasure to do what I can to serve my fellow brothers and sisters. For Jesus Himself taught that whatever we do for the benefit of those who are in need, we also do for Him.[48]

---

[48] Matthew 25:40 – The King will reply, 'I tell you the truth, whatever you did for one of the least of these brothers of mine, you did for me.

19. The Ambassador

Life Lesson: The apple doesn't fall far from the tree.

When I was growing up, I used to watch the television series Kung-Fu staring David Carradine. I was fascinated with how someone could exhibit so much self-control, humility, and respect for other people and things. I knew this was something that I wanted for my own life, so I joined the martial arts and began to study. When I started, I naively thought that all martial artists behaved like Carradine's character, Kwai Chang Caine. However, this notion was quickly shattered after I attended a few tournaments. I'd like to say that the majority of martial artists at these tournaments modeled good behavior, but as is often the case, a few spoil it for the many. The few that stick in my mind demonstrated poor sportsmanship by acting arrogantly, uncontrollably, and disrespectfully.

What's most disheartening is that some of the worst offenders have been black belts. On more than one occasion, I observed instructors actually shouting and brawling with each other during the competition. What would *Master Po*[49] have to say about that one? As a young budding martial artist and an impressionable adolescent lad, I can tell you that it sure disillusioned me. Here I was involved in an art that was supposed to be one of the finest examples of moral character, and instead, I was witnessing many students and instructors alike who had no concern for upholding the standards and ideals of the martial arts. Winning took priority, and there were many who would do anything to walk out the door with the largest number of trophies.

As I attended more and more tournaments, I was able to meet people, recognize faces, and gather information about which students, instructors, clubs, and organizations were

---

[49] Master Po – a character in the old television show, *Kung-Fu*.

connected with each other. I found interesting correlations between students who behaved poorly and their instructors who had similar dispositions. Have you ever heard of the expression, "The apple doesn't fall far from the tree?" Although it usually applies to the ways in which children are likely to mimic their parents and take on much of their learned behavior, I think this saying can apply quite appropriately to the relationship between teachers and their students. Students quite often look up to their teachers and end up following in their footsteps.

A master I trained with once told me that you can usually trace a student's behavior through the patch on his uniform. Wearing a patch with an organization's name or insignia is a way of proclaiming that you belong to and represent that particular group. What some people don't realize is that even though we might not actually wear patches in our daily lives, we all represent who and what we are connected with in life. If someone has one bad experience with a police officer, then he is likely to think that the whole squad is awful. If he has a run-in with a gang of thugs belonging to a particular race, then he is likely to stereotype everybody from that race to possess similar qualities.

Ideally, each person should be judged by his/her own behaviors. Realistically, we are judged by the groups in which we belong. When I go out into the world and people learn that I'm a student at Concordia University, they (consciously or not) formulate opinions about the university based on what they see from me. When I go out into the world and people learn that I'm a martial artist, they (consciously or not) formulate opinions about the martial arts based on what they see from me. It's a heavy burden that we carry, but like it or not, we are all ambassadors because we represent much more than ourselves. Knowing this, we should carefully consider our behaviors on a daily basis.

Similar to the patches that martial artists wear, we as Christians also display symbols that publicly identify a connection that we have with Jesus Christ. Often we wear crosses, rings, t-shirts, and hats which clue people into the ties we have with the Lord. Whether we wear a bracelet that says "WWJD," display a bumper sticker, or glue a fish to the back of our pick-up truck, we are shouting out a bold statement about our beliefs. We're informing others that we are members in God's family. These gestures can be great tools in which to both witness our faith and to strike up a conversation about the Good News Christ has to offer.

Nevertheless, we need to be careful about our speech and actions when we're displaying these symbols in public. What kind of message do you think it sends people when they see the driver of a car sporting a cross decal in the window and flipping off the driver of another vehicle? What sort of message do you think it sends folks who see a person wearing a "Jesus Saves" t-shirt and spilling filthy obscenities out of his mouth? In 2 Corinthians 5:20[50], we see that we are Christ's ambassadors. This is not only a fact, but also a responsibility. I must admit that in the past I've had to think once or twice about my own actions in public.

Now, just because you're not wearing a Christian symbol doesn't give you an excuse to behave any way you please. Let's not forget that a symbol is only a small portion of how we represent ourselves. It's not just a matter of when the WWJD shirt is on, I act all *Christian*-like; and as soon as the shirt comes off, my immoral behavior is unlocked and set free. We must be in a constant state of awareness that everything we do represents who we are in our relationship with Christ. We don't need a physical emblem in order to represent God. As Christians, we all bear the *mark of Christ*.

Even something as simple as words can be symbols to people. Believe me, if you simply exemplify selfless and

---

[50] 2 Corinthians 5:20 – We are therefore Christ's ambassadors, as though God were making His appeal through us. We implore you on Christ's behalf: Be reconciled to God.

loving actions in your everyday behaviors around others, they'll notice something different about you. If they don't already associate your behaviors to the higher group that you belong, then they'll probably at least want to know more about it. They'll follow the trail, not of your patch, but of your conduct and character, and soon discover the Grand Master (Jesus Christ) behind the scenes. Just think, you may even get the chance to introduce the Lord to someone who doesn't know Him. As His ambassador, people will see what Jesus is like through you and the apple will not be far from the tree.

20. Takers and Givers

Life Lesson: It is every man's [and woman's] obligation to put back into the world at least the equivalent of what he takes out of it. ~ Albert Einstein

Let me begin by giving inspirational credit for this next chapter to Dr. Mark Blanke. I was moved to write this after listening to him speak at a conference for youth ministers held in San Antonio, Texas in January, 2003. His message titled "Resource and Recipient" was very insightful.

- -

I've spent quite a number of years giving myself to USA Martial Arts as the primary instructor of every dojo we had. This continued up until the year 2000 when I moved to Austin, Texas to pursue the pastoral ministry. If there's one thing I discovered on this journey, it's that an organization won't work properly if it is nourished by only one person. For years, I became frustrated, because I seemed to be the only continual source of strength in the organization. Sure, there were many others who contributed to its growth, but too much of its existence revolved around me, and I felt like folks were expecting me to be the core.

This situation was not what I had in mind when I founded the organization. I had hopes that the organization would become self-sustaining with multiple key players who shared in both the responsibilities, as well as in the glories and privileges. After I realized that the structure of *USA Martial Arts* was probably not going to change while I was present, I made provisions for a radical transformation. I wanted and needed to do something to ensure that others would share the vision, take hold of the dream, and step up to the plate to bat. Therefore, I slowly began to turn over my schools, one by one, to my black belts so they could teach their own classes.

First, I tried to turn over the schools while living in the area, but it didn't work very well. So, I decided to leave. I turned over the balance of my schools to my black belts, moved from Pennsylvania to Texas, and waited to see what happened. I pushed them out of the nest and allowed them to fly on their own, in hopes that they would grow bigger and stronger. Not everything went as smoothly as I had hoped; however, when I visited, I noticed positive changes were beginning to take place. My hope is that this chapter will inspire you as an individual to stand up for things you're associated with in your own life and make a difference by positively influencing the future of the groups to which you belong.

As we move through stages in our lives, we receive and give in different proportions and to different degrees. Beginning martial arts students mostly receive. I say "mostly" because they are probably contributing financially in a small way. However, as students progress in martial arts, it is expected that they will contribute more than just financially. After maturing, students should be a resource to the school, association, and other students. Martial arts schools can't be complete without assistance in replenishing their resources, and they rely on students eventually giving back as much or more than they've received.

The majority of the higher-ranking belts who leave the dojo do so because they are too focused on taking and not willing to make the transition to give. Many have the attitude of "What's in it for me?" When students focus less on what they can take and more on what they can contribute, things tend to run a lot smoother. There are many ways that students can give. Physically, they can help to improve the condition of the school (cleaning, maintenance, fixing, etc.). Mentally, they can share their wisdom (teaching, assisting others, etc.). Emotionally, they can display pride in their school, talk to others about it, and be a positive example.

Think back to when you were young, to a time when you were but a child and very dependent on Mom and Dad. Your parents did everything for you and gave you everything you needed. This was all good for a while. However, there came a time when it was necessary for you to give back to the family. This is a sign of great maturity and is vital for families to continue to function. Everyone knows that, if mom is the only one in the house doing all the work, things won't continue to go well for long. At some point, she's going to snap. As the saying goes, "If momma isn't happy, nobody's happy." All members of a family system should help to ensure peace and harmony within the unit.

Our spiritual life is similar. Scripture teaches us that God is love, we are helpless (and hopeless) without Him, and Jesus sacrificed everything to provide for our spiritual and eternal salvation. As spiritual beings, God created us not just to take selfishly, but also to turn around and give. This *giving* that God has us do isn't for His benefit; He doesn't need our help. He wants us to become *givers* and *resources* because He loves us and knows that giving will benefit us and make us complete. There is something about giving, and doing so unconditionally, that makes us whole.

God encourages us to give in two ways. First, we are to give our worship and praise to Him. Second, we are to share His love and allow His light to shine through us to the rest of the world. It looks similar to the cross with a vertical and horizontal focus. Vertically, we give back to God what He has already given to us and horizontally we give to our fellow brothers and sisters the good things that God would have us share. The secret to true happiness is giving in the sacrificial way that Christ did through the crucifixion. Only through God's *giving*-plan for our lives will we experience a glimpse of what He and His kingdom is really all about. "Lord, thank you for this marvelous opportunity to share your love with others and become sources of light to them."

21. A Radical New Diet

Life Lesson: All you need for complete health is to feed on the bread of the Lord.

Sadly, many people turn to unhealthy and unnatural methods when it comes to losing weight. In fact, my own past is stained with eating disorders. When I was in my early teens, I starved myself for days at a time and made myself vomit after many meals. I truly believed that I was fat even though the scale read a mere 67 pounds. A couple of decades later I realized that the true root of my disorder was a dislike of myself and a shortage of self-esteem. I thank God for introducing me to the martial arts and for allowing karate to provide me with motivation necessary to pull me out of self-destruction. I now know that the Lord doesn't want us to starve ourselves. He made our bodies dependent on good foods for nourishment, but also for pleasure and enjoyment.

Fasting for the sake of spiritual renewal and clarity is very different than starving your body out of selfish desire. Fasting isn't commanded (look at Mark 2:18[51]), but in reading the Bible you'll find that it's certainly expected (Matthew 6:16-17[52]). When we read about fasting in the Bible, it's usually connected with a spiritual journey. Jesus even fasted in the desert for forty days while being tempted by Satan (Luke 4:4[53]). His fasting was accompanied by some

---

[51] Mark 2:18 – Now John's disciples and the Pharisees were fasting. Some people came and asked Jesus, "How is it that John's disciples and the disciples of the Pharisees are fasting, but yours are not?"

[52] Matthew 6:16-17 – When you fast, do not look somber as the hypocrites do, for they disfigure their faces to show men they are fasting. I tell you the truth, they have received their reward in full. But when you fast, put oil on your head and wash your face.

[53] Luke 4:4 – Jesus answered, "It is written: 'Man does not live on bread alone.'"

intense and spiritually trying times. Nonetheless, Christ resisted those temptations and proved Himself victorious (Romans 5:19[54]).

Lent is a forty-day period of self-denial in which we give up something in order to remember Christ's suffering (and being victorious in that suffering) for us. Fasting is also mentioned in Scripture as a way to enhance our spiritual life along with prayer (Daniel 9:3[55]) by forcing us to deny our physical desires. It's not that God doesn't want us to eat and enjoy the food He's given us, it's that we have to take time every once in a while to realize what's most important in life. To depend on food for our bodies more than we depend on God is unhealthy. Doing so means that we rely on the Creation more than we rely on the Creator.

As with all things, moderation is the key. If your fasting becomes too frequent, begins to get out of hand, or ends up having negative medical consequences, then you've taken it too far, and God's purpose is not sustained. In addition, fasting should be a voluntary act in response to God's love and sacrifice for us, not an obligation or mandate. It shouldn't be drudgery, but rather spiritually uplifting. Certainly fasting should never be performed for dieting. Don't spoil something that is meant to bring you into a closer relationship with God and use it for worldly purposes. Fasting can be a great tool, but only if it's used properly (Acts 14: 22-24[56]).

---

[54] Romans 5:19 – For just as through the disobedience of the one man the many were made sinners, so also through the obedience of the one man the many will be made righteous.

[55] Daniel 9:3 – So I turned to the Lord God and pleaded with Him in prayer and petition, in fasting, and in sackcloth and ashes.

[56] Acts 14:22-24 – "We must go through many hardships to enter the kingdom of God," [the disciples] said. Paul and Barnabas appointed elders

Another way we misuse our God-given gifts is to reject healthy and natural methods for new, "revolutionary" miracle foods and drugs that supposedly make us younger, thinner, and stronger for worldly purposes. Not only are we continually looking for new diets and ways to get fit, we are searching for secular answers that will bring healing and wholeness to our lives. We turn to counseling, therapy, and reading the NY Times bestsellers. However, the extra effort, time, and expense we go through to find out what's wrong in our lives, and how to fix it, can be a little embarrassing when we find out that the solution was right under our noses and readily available to us the whole time.

You may have already heard this story, but once upon a time, there was a good Samaritan who stopped along the side of the road to help a stranded motorist. The motorist was under his car with tools and engine parts spread out all over the place. The stranded motorist said that he had been trying to fix his car all day. After helping the man reassemble the engine and put his tools away, the good Samaritan got in the front seat and tried to start it up. It was then that he noticed the gauge on the dashboard. The stranded motorist was more than embarrassed to learn that he was simply out of gas! My thought is that maybe in life we are simply out of God.

If you are reading this book and don't know what else to do to get your life back on track, then take this advice. Fill up your life's gas tank with God. Our Lord was the only one to walk this earth and not become twisted and defiled by sin. He is the untainted Truth (John 14:6[57]). Don't make things harder on yourself than they need to be by looking in all the wrong places. Through God's Word, found in the Bible, the Holy Spirit can guide you to a fulfilling life of utilizing God's gifts in the ways in which they were originally intended. The

---

for them in each church and, with prayer and fasting, committed them to the Lord, in whom they had put their trust.

[57] John 14:6 – I am the way and the truth and the life.

answer is found in the one who calls Himself the true bread of life (John 6:35[58]). Feed on the only meal that will sustain you throughout life everlasting. Feed on Jesus Christ: our Lord and our provider.

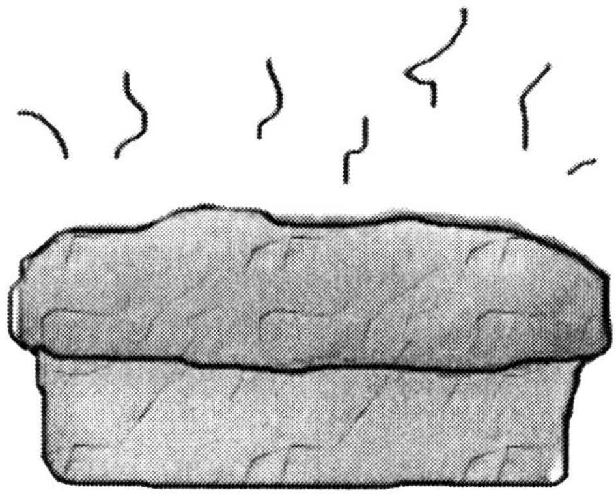

[58] John 6:35 – Then Jesus declared, "I am the bread of life. He who comes to me will never go hungry, and he who believes in me will never be thirsty.

22. Seek the Highest Motive

Life Lesson: A paradigm shift can transform wretchedness into righteousness and make a blind man see.

I once heard a story about a man who was driving his brand new car home from the dealership. As he approached a sharp curve, another vehicle came head-on from around the corner swerving into his lane. Luckily, the woman who was driving towards him was able to jerk her car back into her own lane at the last minute thus avoiding a collision. As she passed him, she stuck her head out the window and yelled at him, "Fat Pig!" Infuriated, the man instinctively shouted back, "Old Cow!" Just seconds later, the man continued around the corner and wrecked his brand new car after running into a huge boar that was standing directly in his path.

A paradigm is a pre-conceived notion that we carry with us. Paradigms usually cause us to impose our views and opinions without knowing the facts, leading us to act or react in some particular fashion. As we can see from the story about the "Fat Pig," the man had a completely different idea in mind when the woman shouted at him. Maybe he carries baggage with him from the past, which led him to assume that people are naturally mean. Maybe he's had some women in his life that have treated him badly. Or possibly, he just always assumes the worst in people. For whatever reason, he clearly misunderstood the woman's intentions and jumped to the wrong conclusion.

Not only did he ruin his brand new car because he jumped to the wrong conclusion, but he could have really hurt the woman who tried to help him. Who knows what being called an "Old Cow" might have done. What if it was the last straw for her and she'll never go out of her way to help others again. It's scary to think about the chain reactions that our words and behaviors might potentially cause in the lives of others. How often have we said or done negative things that had lasting effects on people? Unnecessary pain is inflicted because we sometimes don't take the time to see another's point of view. Just think of the agony we could spare if we would take time to understand our own and other people's paradigms.

In the martial arts, we consider our paradigms very carefully. Making assumptions or even taking things for granted in a self-defense situation can be hazardous to your health. Paradigms in relationships should also be considered carefully. Making negative assumptions or not taking time to understand the paradigms that exist in a situation can destroy some relationships. When in doubt, it is always best to seek the highest motive. If someone offers you a suggestion as to how you can do something better, take it as a compliment. Don't just assume that the person is manipulative and controlling. Consider that the person is trying to be helpful and wants you to grow.

Even Jesus knew about and was subject to paradigms. It was He who said a prophet isn't accepted in his own town (Luke 4:24[59]), and He was right. It wasn't a group of total strangers that crucified Jesus, it was His own people! I'm sure it must have been hard for the people who grew up with Jesus to see Him as the Savior. After all, would you ever believe the son of your local carpenter to be the Savior of the world? In addition to the *hometown* factor, many of the town's people had a certain paradigm of what the savior would be like, and Jesus didn't fit the bill. His people were looking for a strong leader who would conquer their enemies in the physical world. They wanted someone who would raise up an army to make them rulers of the land. They weren't expecting someone who would humble Himself to the point of death in order to combat the forces of the spiritual world.

---

[59] Luke 4:24 – I tell you the truth, He continued, No prophet is accepted in his hometown.

It is only through Jesus that we can experience true transformation of the sinful paradigms we acquire from this sinful world, and can therefore be set free to new possibilities. When you choose to seek the highest motive, you're choosing to seek Jesus Christ Himself. You set aside your preconceived human notions and build faith in something higher. You don't allow your lack of self-esteem and your worldly experiences to define the way you see people and things. Instead, you see them the way Jesus did; "Father, forgive them; for they know not what they do" (Luke 23:34). Even in sinful humanity, Jesus sought the highest motive. It is only through Christ that we can experience a paradigm shift that changes our path from wretched to righteous, and allows us to see the light. It is only through Him that we can even begin to learn what it means to seek the highest motive.

23. Testing, Testing

Life Lesson: Tests help us learn; even awful tests can result in something positive.

One of the biggest fears that students harbor is test taking. The very mention of the word "test" can send some students into a panic. This high anxiety can cause them to sweat, feel nauseous, and sometimes even lose all train of thought. As a martial arts instructor, one of my goals is to help students learn how to deal with this anxiety. After all, most physical confrontations are ridden with anxiety. If we don't learn to deal with it eventually, then it could result in some serious trouble in the future.

Learning how to fearlessly take tests isn't only for martial arts students. Anxiety control is useful in multiple areas of our lives. There are literally thousands of different tests available: driving tests, placement tests, certification tests, and more. We take tests in school and at work, as well as to get into schools and to acquire work. Tests are necessary for us to advance and grow, and as long as we plan to move up in life, we should never expect to get away from them.

As a college student, I take an incredible amount of tests. One of the hardest classes is Greek. It's not the testing that is difficult; it's the manner in which the tests are given. You see, the majority are impromptu. In other words, all the students start to panic when the professor begins class by saying, "Take everything off your desk, and get out a blank sheet of paper." Sometimes those very words echo in my dreams and wake me up at night as I scream in terror. What can I do to ease this anguish, subdue my suffering, and pacify the pain?

The best way to learn to deal with the fear of tests is to better understand the fear. My professor has two opinions about test taking. First, he thinks we worry too much when we know a test is coming up; we worry about the test and we worry about how the worry will affect our ability to take the test. Picture an armadillo and a squirrel in the road with a fast moving car approaching. When they see the oncoming car, the two animals react differently. The result…an unscathed squirrel and armadillo soup at the *Road Kill Café*.

The problem wasn't with the car (which represents the upcoming test); the problem was with the way in which one of the animals reacted to the car. Armadillos jump straight up and curl into a ball when they are afraid. If the armadillo hadn't reacted in such a way, it would have probably been okay. Sometimes we make more out of things than we should. Sometimes we cut our own throats by overreacting and jumping to conclusions.

When it comes time to take a test, take it easy, and don't panic. Let "Que Sera, Sera[60]" be your motto. Now I'm not saying, don't plan and prepare; Ben Franklin once said, "By failing to prepare, you're preparing to fail." I'm merely saying don't worry, especially about things that haven't happened yet. Do your best to plan, prepare, and take the test and then let it go. As the saying goes, "whatever will be, will be." Your worrying about it isn't going to make any bit of difference.

My professor's second opinion about taking tests is that it should be just another tool in the learning process. Tests help us to figure out what we know and what we still need to learn. If our primary objective is to learn, then we shouldn't cringe at the mention of a test. If we were truly concerned about learning, then we'd be saying, "Hurray for the test," and "Yippee, we get to take another." We'd be thankful and happily rejoice at the opportunity to better measure what we know and still need to know.

Instead, we want to slump down in our desks and hide our faces in shame. Why do we act this way? Because we're more concerned about our *appearing* to be smart than our actually *becoming* smart. We want our instructors (and other

---

[60] Que Sera, Sera – Spanish phrase for "whatever will be, will be."

classmates) to think highly of us more than we care about knowing the truth. Doing poorly on a test doesn't affect our learning, it affects our façade. Our ego can really get in the way of our learning, if we let it. Contrary to the way we feel, exposing our weaknesses can be extremely beneficial in the learning process.

I pray that I'll always be able to let down this façade as the pastor of a congregation. I never want my time and effort to be wrapped up in getting people to think highly of me. Sure, some people may think highly of me because of certain things I do, but that shouldn't be my reason for doing them. When I stand in front of the congregation delivering my sermons, I'll be much more effective when I can put aside the worries of how I look. I just need to remember that it's not all about me!

While descending from his pulpit after an excellent sermon, Charles H. Spurgeon was told by members of his congregation that he was a great preacher. His reply was, "Yes, the devil has already told me that." Being a good pastor (or being a good parent, public servant, teacher, or whatever) is to put others needs ahead of your own. As a pastor, I must always think of what is best for my parishioners, and as a teacher, I must always think of what is best for my students. My Greek professor said it best, "With years of experience, you'll eventually be able to do this for seconds at a time." Wow, what wonderful insight!

Contrary to what some people believe, it's not the Lord who is tempting us to put on this façade, but one who is called the tempter (Matthew 4:3)[61]: Satan. While I do not think that Satan is good in any way, shape, or form, good things can come from our encounters with him (if we are operating in the presence of the Lord), as well as from sin that is repented and forgiven. Good things can also come from

---

[61] Matthew 4:3 – The tempter came to Him and said, "If you are the Son of God, tell these stones to become bread."

natural disasters that happen in the world. God is able to turn any bad thing around and use it for His Holy purpose. For example, I have a friend whose house burned down. Now, God didn't burn it down; however, He did use the situation to place Christian people in my friend's life who would later point him towards Christ. He now has a deeper appreciation for the things in life (not material) that are truly important.

If we choose, we can think of Satan as being here to do a job. His job is not to simply point out our weaknesses and faults; it's to get us riled up about being imperfect. Yes, it'd be better if he weren't here; however, as long as he is, let's see how we can make the best of it. When we see flaws in ourselves, we can recognize our need for improvement rather than get riled up about them. After all, we can't see that our house is infested with termites until some of the exterior is pulled away to reveal the truth underneath. So let's be thankful that our exterior (façade) is pulled off from time to time. After all, without Satan testing me and showing me my faults, I might not have ever seen a need for God.

I'm so thankful for God's light (Jesus Christ). By this powerful light, I can see all the dark areas in my life that don't measure up to God's will. He's the perfect answer key to the test. It's only by comparing ourselves to Jesus that we realize what areas in our lives need improvement. Now, we are able to walk more closely with Christ and develop that deep relationship which He wants with every one of us. We no longer have to waste time hiding from Him because we know that He is aware of all our faults and wants us anyway. It's as if Jesus took each of our tests and gave everyone a perfect score even though He knew that we didn't actually deserve it. He wrote in big red letters across the top of each exam, "A+ 100%." By trusting in Christ for our eternal salvation, there will be no such thing as failure.

24. What's that Smell?

Life Lesson: Our road to cleanliness is recognizing that something stinks, admitting that it's us, and allowing the stench to be wiped away.

Throughout my martial arts career, I've noticed many of my students on the sidelines when they should be out on the workout floor. Subconsciously they are probably thinking, "As long as I don't place myself out there for everyone to see, I can keep up this charade of being faultless." It seems a little backwards, but I've noticed that those who need to practice the most are usually the most reluctant in class. Don't they know that we all need to learn and improve? Don't they understand that nobody is perfect and we all make mistakes all the time? I suspect that their first priority is not to learn martial arts, but rather to do whatever possible to ensure that others have a high opinion of them.

I think that all of us have put on charades of one form or another in different areas of our lives. Possibly, it's lying to our acquaintances in order to make ourselves seem great. Perhaps we embellish our stories so that people will like us. For some of us it's the accumulation of material things and financial wealth so that we can entertain our friends. We might be reluctant to open up and be ourselves because we're afraid of not being accepted. Whether we engage in this behavior at work, school, or even at home, it takes great effort to keep up our charades and keep others from seeing and knowing our true selves. It's sad to think about how much time and energy we put into covering up, when we could be putting it into being the person God created us to be.

Although it's true that some people will maliciously (and others, accidentally) trample on our hearts when we open and expose the tender areas of our lives, I do know of someone who would never do such a thing. I know someone who cares for us so deeply that He accepts us as we are. God knows our innermost secrets, and He's familiar with the undisclosed realities of our lives. There is no door we can lock and there are no blinds to close that can keep Him from knowing the truth about us. The amazing thing is that even though God knows us inside and out and is well aware of our many shortcomings, He still wants to be our Father. Wow, that's love!

Consider the following idea from a fellow classmate by the name of Neil Vanderbush: *God purifies us when we have a poopy diaper*. Some of us live our lives like toddlers in potty training that crap their pants. God, our Father, of course notices the smell right away. How could He not? Anyone who has ever spent time around young children, who have accidents, knows that the smell is impossible to hide. It's kind of like the story of Adam and Eve in the Garden of Eden. In Genesis 3, they hid from God because they knew that they were naked. God called out, "Where are you?" even though He knew very well where they were.

God asks us questions not because He doesn't know the answers, but because He wants us to stop covering up and face the truth. Just like when a father asks, "What's that smell?" he knows very well what that smell is and where it is coming from, he just wants to call attention to it, to have his toddler acknowledge it and fess up, especially if the toddler is in potty training. In asking us questions, God is inviting us to have a dialog with Him and trust in Him to admit our guilt. He is offering to clean us up and send us on our merry way, even knowing that He'll have to do so again and again.

Unfortunately, we as sinners often run and hide. "I think someone's had an accident," a father might say. The child responds from across the room (trying to keep as far away from the father as possible), "It's not me." As adults, do we really believe that God doesn't know the smell is coming from us, or are we just trying to convince ourselves that our poop doesn't stink? After all, we know when we mess up. What we don't often understand is that our loving father just wants us to be clean. He knows the pain and suffering of the rash that results when we decide to stay dirty.

Even though we won't go to Him, He comes over to us and picks us up in His gentle arms. He won't turn His back in anger and spite because we were supposed to know better than to mess ourselves. Instead, He cleans us up as one who is faithful and just, and in the end (pun intended), we feel much better. Every time we mess up, dad simply picks us up, discards the dirty diaper, and wipes us clean. To boot, He even gives us a big hug and tells us how much He loves us before putting us back down and allowing us to go on with the rest of our day. Soon, after lots of repetition, we begin to learn of His faithfulness. We learn to trust and take confidence in His love. Eventually we even start coming to dad on our own and telling Him when we've made a mess of things.

Our Father has nothing but the best of intentions for us. If we truly trust in Him, and know that there's nothing that we can hide from Him, it's no big deal to go to Him for help. Sometimes, we're incapable of cleaning up our own messes. So, we stand at His feet with outstretched arms and wait for Him to pick us up and make us and our pants clean again. He wants us to come to Him willingly and He swiftly embraces us as we do. Facing the truth of our messes and admitting our guilt, even though we're supposed to know better, is the only way for us to be cleaned up, and it is the only way we can learn from our mistakes and grow up.

The next step in growing up is to recognize the signs of when we're about to mess ourselves. If we can recognize the signs that this terrible thing is about to happen, then we can stop pooping in our pants. There's a certain feeling that we all get when it's about to happen. The more honest we are with ourselves and the more aware we become of the feeling, the more we avoid those "accidents" in our lives. However, as the skid-marks in my shorts will testify, accidents do and will happen. Some are worse than others are, and I don't get them nearly as often as I used to, but none of us will ever outgrow them completely.

As we become Christians and mature in our faith, the cycle of not wanting to admit our guilt starts all over again. People have higher standards for us and expect that we will live up to them without any problems. It's five hundred times more embarrassing to poop your pants as an adult than it was when you were a toddler. Everyone assumes that you must be completely potty-trained as you grow up. One fear that I have about becoming a pastor is that people will try to hold me to an unrealistically high standard of being perfect and sinless.

Now, I know that I should live a clean life. However, will people forgive me when I screw up? Or will they, as so many do, call me a hypocrite and shun me? I don't mind telling you, I'm scared! I'm not at the point yet in my life where I don't care about other's opinions of me. Can I do it? I don't know. I do know that I can place my trust in the arms of my Heavenly Father who picks me up daily, wipes me clean, and puts me back down with a gentle kiss. I don't have to worry about living up to any certain standard with Him. I just have to admit my imperfections and mistakes by confessing.

I also pray that I'll have the same understanding and forgiveness that I desire when I encounter others who have made mistakes in their lives. I pray that I won't ever laugh at their faults, point at their imperfections, or talk about them behind their backs. I pray most of all that I won't ever turn my back on any of my fellow brothers or sisters who may happen to have the same smelly odor of sin coming from the seat of their pants as I do. For I have learned that everyone's poop stinks and everyone needs to be cleaned from time to time.

25. What's in a Title?

Life Lesson: Respect is about recognizing the value of others and honoring the relationships that connect us all.

One thing that I struggled with for many years is the use of titles in the karate school. While it's actually expected by the majority of martial artists that students will address their instructors by a title such as "Sensei"[62] or "Shihan"[63] to show them respect in the karate school, many believe that it is inappropriate for these titles to be carried outside the karate school. They believe that when students meet their instructors on the *street*, they should just call them Bob or Sue. Because we are all created equal, they believe that if anyone uses a title outside of the confines of the place in which the title is generally associated, then he/she is being arrogant and self-absorbed.

Furthermore, I've had people question our use of "Master" as a title; citing Matthew 23:8[64] from the Wycliffe New Testament (2001) by Terrence P. Noble. I must admit that I've lost a lot of sleep over this controversial issue; however, I'm now convinced that there's nothing wrong with using our society's titles outside of the classroom. Some translations of the Bible do say that no man should be called "master," but after studying Greek (the language originally used to write the New Testament), I found that the word "Master" isn't used at all. What it does say is that no man is to be called "teacher" or "father."

---

[62] Sensei – A Japanese word that is used as a title for any black belt instructor in the arts.

[63] Shihan – A Japanese word that is used as a title for a person with a master's degree in the martial arts.

[64] Matthew 23:8 – But do not ye be called master; for one is your master, and all ye be brethren (taken from the Wycliffe New Testament, 2001, by Terrence P. Noble).

Nonetheless, even literal translations must be taken in context. The Bible doesn't mean that we shouldn't refer to the individuals who aid our learning process as "teachers." And it certainly doesn't mean that it's wrong to refer to the male parent in your life as "father." What it means is that God is our ultimate teacher and our Father in Heaven; it warns against equating human beings with The Almighty. In fact, I refer to the man who sired me as father. There is nothing wrong with this because I don't worship him like my Heavenly Father. I merely show him respect as the Bible commands us to do in Exodus 20:12[65].

It's quite common for our society to call people by the titles in which we relate to them, even outside of their usual domain. This is a sign of respect. For example, I don't call my father by his first name just because we happen to be outside of the home. When I run into my old teachers from grade school and especially my college professors in the grocery store, I still call them "Mr. Johnson", and "Professor Phillips". Does anyone else out there besides me still call his or her physician, "Doctor ______?" Now, if your dad were a professor, you probably wouldn't call him Dr. so and so... because he's your dad, not your professor. Relationships are what order the titles we use... not physical locations.

It isn't appropriate to use titles outside of the scope of the relationship that you have with people. If you are not a martial arts student, and you do not associate yourself with the martial arts, then there's no reason why you should call me "Master Brown." If a person is using a title outside of the scope of its appropriate relationship, then it is nothing more than an ego-booster. After all, the relationship is what makes the title an appropriate form of respect for the addressee. Without the relationship, the title is meaningless to the addressee. It is here where a title can become a dangerous

[65] Exodus 20:12 – "Honor your father and your mother, so that you may live long in the land the LORD your God is giving you."

trap of pride that some people fall into and sink in their own mire.

Why then do I advocate the use of titles if they carry the potential to have negative consequences? It's because they have some positive effects too; and those positive effects outweigh the negative. Titles actually benefit the people who use them much more than the people who hold them. As a teacher, it's my job to give students what I think they need, and I think students need to learn respect, especially since our culture seems to foster quite the opposite. While using a title doesn't guarantee respect, it's certainly a step in the right direction and every step counts. However, like seeds planted in the ground (see 1 Corinthians 3:6[66]), there's no guarantee seeds of respect will grow, or that I'll be around when the growth begins. It is only God who makes seeds grow and I must remember that He is in complete control.

Respect helps us in many ways. It helps us to maintain and appreciate the relationships we have with others, it keeps us humble, and it encourages us to grow outward in community instead of inward as isolated individuals. By respecting others, we honor God because we display love for our neighbor and uphold the structure of society that He has given us for social order and continuity. We recognize individuals for their contributions to the world and encourage one another to continue in service to all. We show people that they have intrinsic value as children of God, and expresses reverence toward the Creator. Whether you demonstrate respect by using appropriate titles, through your actions, or simply by the words you speak, it makes no difference. They are all worthy ways of recognizing the value of others and honoring the relationships that connect us all.

---

[66] 1 Corinthians 3:6 – I planted the seed, Apollos watered it, but God made it grow.

26. Let it Be

Life Lesson: Give a man a fish and you'll feed him for a day... but teach a man to fish and you'll feed him for a lifetime.

In working with students, it is very important to know the difference between giving them what they want, what you want, and what they truly need. Far too often I have to steer my apprentice instructors away from giving students what they as instructors want. It's easier to give students the right answers than it is to help them discover the answers on their own. Yes, it's much more valuable for students to discover than to be spoon-fed. As teachers, we can become very impatient and quick to move ahead with our own agendas even though we know a student isn't ready yet. Giving a man a fish is easy, but you only feed him for a day. Teaching a man to fish takes more time, but you feed him for a lifetime.

I've seen this kind of impatience in several different families. Time after time (not just an isolated incident) I've noticed parents putting their own agendas ahead of their kids. One of the hardest things to do as a parent is to discipline your child. I remember as if it were yesterday the first time I ever spanked my son. The old cliché, "This is going to hurt me more than it hurts you" comes to mind. Of course, we're talking about two completely different kinds of pain. His pain was a stinging physical pain on the surface of his butt, but mine was a dull heartache squeezing and twisting deep down inside. Most parents will testify that they'd do almost anything to prevent their children from suffering.

On the other hand, sparing your child from suffering isn't always in the child's best interest. We must sometimes do the uncomfortable thing and be strong to discipline a child. Likewise, we must sometimes be self-controlled and not react out of anger. Controlled discipline is good teaching, but an uncontrolled reaction can borderline abusive behavior. I can't warn strongly enough against disciplining on the tip of our emotions. If we don't control our emotions, they'll control us. Disciplining should always be done out of love (in the child's best interest) and certainly with plenty of self-control on the parent's part. When emotions heat up, we should take time out and resume a more controlled approach to discipline later.

When our emotions control our discipline, we can be too harsh or too lenient. This rollercoaster-ride approach to dealing with kids teaches them how to and how not to drive the parent's emotions. In other words, it doesn't teach them anything constructive. I know of a few families that are constantly bailing their kids out of trouble instead of allowing them to experience the natural consequences of their actions. Maybe a child leaves his comic books outside in the lawn (knowing he's not supposed to), and then it rains and his comic books are ruined. Do you tell him, "It's okay honey, I'll buy you some new comic books tomorrow," or do you listen to his pain and say, "I'm sorry to hear that happened"? How you respond will determine what he does next time.

In any case, there's no sense in getting mad at him. Simply allow the boy to take some responsibility for his own mistakes and learn from his faults. You may offer or help him find a way that he can earn some money to buy himself some more comic books. Conversely, if the books are simply replaced for him the next day, all he's learning is that life doesn't offer consequences and he can be as irresponsible as he wants to be because someone else will always be there to bail him out of trouble. I know of a family where the kids are older and "on their own," but the parents are continuously giving their kids money to pay their bills. Essentially, the parents are paying for their two kids (both around the age of twenty) to live out on their own.

I'm not against parents helping their kids financially. I'm grateful that my parents helped me out in the past. However, there is a difference between giving kids some cash because they've met hard times and enabling them to be dependent on their parents. When two kids are out on their own but can't seem to hold down a steady job, then there's a problem with their self-help skills. In essence, they don't know how (or don't want to know how) to take care of themselves. They have money for extras (tobacco, movies, and snacks), but their phone has just been shut off and one of them is about to have his car repossessed by the bank. What do they do? They call mommy and daddy for help.

Here's where it gets tough for mom and dad. Mom and dad have to buckle down, do the difficult thing, and tell their kids, "No!" I didn't know this family when the kids were young, but I imagine that these parents may have also caved in to their children's complaining and whining just to shut the little buggers up. Is giving in to your kids, for a moment of peace and quiet, in their best interest or yours? If parents aren't careful, kids will learn how to use this tactic to their advantage and this behavior won't be outgrown easily. In most cases, it will follow children right into adulthood, which is what happened in the example of the two kids.

Now, I know that the parents only want the best for their kids (or so they say). They tell me that they can't bear to watch them go hungry or have their stuff taken away. I say let the kids experience the natural consequences of their own decisions in life and maybe they'll mature in the process. Let the 20-year-old experience what its like to go hungry for a day or to actually have his utilities shut off and you'll see how committed he becomes to keeping one of those many jobs he goes through. Certainly, it's difficult, but that's where tough love comes in. It's the same kind of heart-wrenching pain that we go through when it's time to spank our kids. It's not fun, it's not easy, but we do it for their benefit, even though they don't like it at the time.

Conversely, having no discipline always feels good at the time, but in the long term, it's unbearably painful. I heard about a cartoon on a theologian's door that depicts Satan greeting people in Hell and saying: "You'll find that there's no right or wrong here, just what works for you." The fruit of an undisciplined life seems sugary sweet at first, but you'll find that it rots to the core in no time flat. Thus, we as parents need to put aside our own feelings of guilt and short-term discomfort for a greater feeling of love and long-term benefits for our children. Parents, help your kids grow and become responsible adults who know the value of accepting the consequences for their own decisions in life.

A man once saw a butterfly struggling to get out of its chrysalis[67]. He went over and, taking pity on it, he cracked open the walls of the structure to make life easier on the little fellow. He thought he was giving the creature what it needed. His intentions were good, but indeed, he was actually sentencing the butterfly to death. Because it hadn't had the proper time to develop, or gain the muscle strength necessary, it couldn't fly. The butterfly was crippled and defenseless. In no time, it became the supper of one of its predators. Let me now give you something to ponder. How many times do we crack open the shells of the people we love, making their immediate life easier, but sentencing them to unforeseen suffering in the long run because we circumvented the crucial development that in the end would have provided victory?

I thank God for allowing us to experience the natural consequences of our actions. I also thank Him for giving us free will to choose our own paths in life. Although I often screw up, like that little boy who left his comic books outside when it rained, I pray that I too will learn from my mistakes and grow as a result. Read the third and fourth verse in the fifth chapter of Romans[68] where Paul teaches that character is strengthened by suffering. By allowing us to struggle, we,

---

[67] Chrysalis – the butterfly's version of (and often confused with) a cocoon which is spun by moths, caterpillars, and certain other insects.

[68] Romans 5:3-4 – Not only so, but we also rejoice in our sufferings, because we know that suffering produces perseverance; perseverance, character; and character, hope.

like the butterfly, develop, become stronger, and learn to spread our wings and fly. We are then ready to go out into the world, face new challenges, and accomplish amazing things instead of being easily swallowed up by our predators. So, with that in mind, let's trust that God knows (and does) what's best for us.

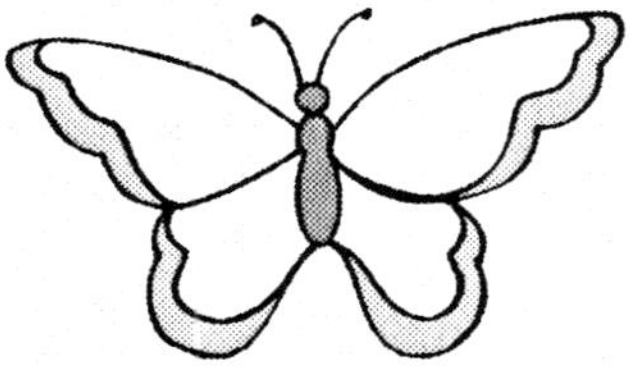

27. Christian Copy Cats

Life Lesson: We can, and are expected to transform the things in this world into things that give honor and glory to God.

Every time martial artists enter or exit the training hall, they are expected to stop and bow towards the hall. This is a tradition that goes back many generations, and is rooted in Eastern culture and religion. While we continue this practice even today, we don't bow because we are engaged in Eastern worship, we bow out of courtesy and respect. Taking non-Christian traditions and using them for a new purpose is okay to do. It's been done throughout centuries by people and even by God. For example, Christmas was originally a pagan festival, not a day to celebrate Christ's birth. Nevertheless, Christians decided adopt December 25th because it was a popular time for *celebration* in the culture in which they lived and they wanted to celebrate Jesus Christ.

Actually, the twist of symbolism that they made in the transition of this festival was quite clever. The celebration was originally set aside for the return of the sun. However, Christians changed its meaning to celebrate the coming of the Son (the birth of Jesus). Similarly, circumcision was around long before God instituted it as a practice for His people to carry out. It was He who gave it a completely new purpose. Moreover, let's not forget the covenant[69] God used on Mount Sinai. The notion of covenant was also already in place and therefore an easy mental transition for His people. Finally, we cannot possibly overlook the crucifixion, which would have never been used for Holy purposes before the death of Jesus. Again, God simply took concepts that were familiar to His people and suited them for a new purpose.

---

[69] The Sinai Covenant was a treaty or agreement with God. The Israelites followed rules that upheld their end of the agreement, and in return, God offered them His care and protection. This was similar to other sovereign treaties used in the same time period between kings and their vassals.

We do the same when we bow in and out of the training hall. We don't bow because we consider the training hall to be a holy place. We bow to recognize and appreciate it as a special place where we train. In essence, bowing in and bowing out is like turning on and off a switch that connects our brains to our training. Our focus is solely on our training from the time we bow in to the time we bow out. We show the training hall respect for this reason and gratitude for all that we learn within its walls. We also show appreciation for having a place in which we can train.

There's another place in which I urge you to show the same amount of respect, gratitude, and appreciation because it, too, is a place of great transformation. It's your body. In 1 Corinthians 3:16[70] and 2 Corinthians 6:16[71] we learn that our bodies are temples of the Lord. Yes, the Holy Spirit lives inside of those who do not reject Him. Because we were born in original sin, our bodies used to be the dwelling place of the devil. However, upon our baptism, the Holy Spirit enters in and exorcises the evil. He claims what was once the property of the devil for His own holy purpose. Knowing this gives a completely new perspective about self-respect. Being that our bodies are not our own, we should care for and treat them as we would valuable pieces of property that are entrusted to us.

Consequently, abusing our bodies with drugs, pre-marital sex, excessive amounts of alcohol, and any other unhealthy behaviors is disrespectful to the Lord and defiles His temple. We owe God and ourselves much more. If you know the Passion Story of Christ, you realize just how much He went through to purchase us back from the evil one. We,

---

[70] 1 Corinthians 3:16 – Don't you know that you yourselves are God's temple and that God's Spirit lives in you?

[71] 2 Corinthians 6:16 – What agreement is there between the temple of God and idols? For we are the temple of the living God. As God has said: "I will live with them and walk among them, and I will be their God, and they will be my people."

who once were worthless, are now priceless treasures! He did so much for our renovation; certainly we know that we are special and deserve only the best. Therefore, I urge you to care for and respect the gifts that God has given to you... mainly your Bodies (His Temple).

Although we, God's children, are certainly the most valuable of all his creation, and are by far His first priority, God isn't content with only the transformation of *our* bodies, minds, and spirits. Everything in His creation should be utilized to fulfill His will and serve His purpose; and we are called to aid in this larger transformation. The things of this world, which were once dead, can be given new life and incredible significance if they become tools to serve the Lord. One such example is the martial arts. This activity can serve several worldly purposes and be very positive, but since we are but *dust*[72] *in the wind*, it cannot take us into eternity. Now if we transform martial arts for God's purposes, then we have a completely new activity that serves the will and work of God! Whether it's a sport, an object, an organization, an action, a tradition, a person, or a place... if it's transformed into a vehicle for carrying out the holy will of our Creator, then Hallelujah–praise be to God!

---

[72] Genesis 3:19 – By the sweat of your brow you will eat your food until you return to the ground, since from it you were taken; for dust you are and to dust you will return.

28. Give Me a Break

Life Lesson: Succeeding in life is like breaking a board; it takes Foundation, Faith, Focus, Fitness, and Follow-through.

One of the most popular activities in the martial arts seems to be breaking objects. I don't think that I would dare do a public demonstration without performing some sort of breaking feat. The crowd wouldn't understand. There's just something exciting about smashing wood or concrete with bare hands and feet. It's not only fun to watch, but fun to do. In fact, it's one of the most popular activities among students, too. Maybe it's the release of aggression into the object that makes it so enjoyable. Or, maybe it's the representation of the object to be broken. These boards and bricks represent many obstacles in our lives, and our breaking through them to the other side means smashing obstacles and achieving success.

To help students understand what it takes to break a board, I recommend mastering "The Five F's" of breaking. These five elements are *Foundation*, *Faith*, *Focus*, *Fitness*, and *Follow-through*. Just as there are five key elements needed to break a board, there are similarly five key elements to breaking through any roadblocks that lie in the path of life. As you learn about what it takes to break a board, I encourage you to apply these elements to other trials that you may be facing. As with breaking a board, it won't be easy, and you may have to make several attempts before you succeed, but I assure you that victory can and will be yours if you can only persevere.

The first thing that we must always consider when attempting a break is *Foundation*. You see there are different kinds of foundations. When the foundation is a person holding a board for someone to break, it is weak. It's tough to break a board this way because a great deal of the energy exerted into breaking the board is absorbed by the give or movement of the foundation, or in this case, the person holding the board. Although a good holder can provide a sufficient foundation, there's no question that there are stronger and better foundations to use in breaking. The easiest way to break a board is by placing it correctly on top of a couple of bricks. When the board is struck, the bricks won't budge. Because the board has been set on a rock-solid foundation, it's a lot easier to break.

How about your foundation in life? Is it strong and secure like the bricks? Are your feet firmly planted? If so, then in what are they planted? Be careful, the world is full of lies and distractions. We can be planted in worldly trends, our own physical strength, or our own wisdom. Maybe we're leaning on someone else (a friend, spouse, or caregiver), or even how much money we have in the bank. If we're planted in these things, then our foundation might as well be shifting sand. Every one of these things (and other worldly things) can be here today and gone tomorrow. The only true foundation that we can be sure of never shifting out from underneath us is Jesus Christ. Read Job 22:15-17[73], Matthew 7:5[74], Luke 6:48[75], and especially Ephesians 2:19-21[76].

---

[73] Job 22:15-17 – Will you keep to the old path that evil men have trod? They were carried off before their time, their foundations washed away by a flood. They said to God, 'Leave us alone! What can the Almighty do to us?'

[74] Matthew 7:5 – The rain came down, the streams rose, and the winds blew and beat against that house; yet it did not fall, because it had its foundation on the rock.

[75] Luke 6:48 – He is like a man building a house, who dug down deep and laid the foundation on rock. When a flood came, the torrent struck that house but could not shake it, because it was well built.

[76] Ephesians 2:19-21 – Consequently, you are no longer foreigners and aliens, but fellow citizens with God's people and members of God's household, built on the foundation of the apostles and prophets, with Christ Jesus Himself as the chief cornerstone. In Him the whole building is joined together and rises to become a holy temple in the Lord.

The second thing that's extremely important when breaking a board (or doing anything in life) is to have strong *Faith.* You must truly believe that you can do something if you expect to ever do it. If you don't believe in yourself, then you probably won't be inclined to try, and if you end up trying just because of peer pressure or something else, then you probably won't accomplish much. Even if you end up trying something and accomplishing it, you probably won't give yourself credit. Instead, you'll call it a fluke or a coincidence. The mind is extremely powerful in not only shaping our actions but in shaping our attitudes about them. Therefore, don't try to accomplish anything that you don't believe you can accomplish.

Third, if you want to be successful, you need to learn to *Focus.* When breaking a board, there are two types of focus. One is *mental focus* and the other is *physical focus.* Mental focus is aiming beyond the object, to the other side. However, physical focus is the art of hitting the object in the exact point necessary to make the break easier. Since a board isn't as likely to break if it is struck near its foundation, we should try to strike the board directly in the center (as far away from its support as possible). Think about the spiritual parallels that this concept has for our lives. If we receive a direct hit far away from our support, which is Christ, then we, like the board, are likely to be snapped in two. Therefore, let us rest completely on the rock we know to be Jesus.

We must all watch where we *focus* our attention. The body will naturally follow the eyes. Ice skaters, ballerinas, and gymnasts use this principle as well as martial artists. I tell my students not to focus on the board itself. The board is the obstacle, and we should never focus on the obstacle. Instead, think only about carrying your hand through to the other side. Concentrate on the goal, what is beyond the obstacle. Often in life I find myself getting too wrapped up in thinking about my problems and all the obstacles that keep me from my goals instead of focusing my attention on where I'm going. In the end, I waste a lot of time and energy that could have been redirected elsewhere towards success.

There are two more principles to successful breaking. The next one has to do with power and *Fitness*. If a fist comes down on a board with only a teaspoon of energy, then the board isn't going to budge. It's a funny thing that breaking a board doesn't hurt much at all if it actually breaks. However, if you strike a board and the board doesn't break, then the power is absorbed right back into the hand and you'll most certainly experience the consequences of only giving 80%. It takes 100% of a person's energy to break an object. However, as embarrassing as it is, even I have recently made the mistake of not putting all my energy into a strike (because of my overconfidence) and have failed.

So, where does this power come from? First, it comes from all the principles. Because each principle hinges on the other, you won't find the required energy if you are without a good foundation, faith, and focus. Second, power is gained by training. It's a very long process, but strength training is extremely important. It's not required that we be muscle-bound, but it does help to be toned and fit. Thankfully when tackling obstacles in our everyday lives, it doesn't take nearly as long to build strength. In fact, strength is available to us immediately without any effort on our part. I'm not talking about muscles, but about Christ. Read Exodus 15:2[77], and Psalm 28:7[78]. With Christ as your strength, you'll be amazed at the power you can possess in life.

The last of the five principles is *Follow-through*. I've seen many students attempt to break boards and not make it

---

[77] Exodus 15:2 – The LORD is my strength and my song; He has become my salvation. He is my God, and I will praise Him, my father's God, and I will exalt Him.

[78] Psalm 28:7 – The LORD is my strength and my shield; my heart trusts in Him, and I am helped. My heart leaps for joy and I will give thanks to Him in song.

because of a lack of follow-through. Their foundation, faith, focus, and fitness level (power exerted) were all top-notch. However, they stopped short when hitting the board. Their strike came down on the board and stopped just as it hit the outer surface. All the power in the world wouldn't have done them any good. Consider a racerunner. If the runner gets all the way to the finish line and focuses on the tape that is strung across the track, he/she is likely to slow down and reduce speed before making contact with it. Instead, the runner focuses beyond the tape, and when she crosses the finish line, she is still running at 100%.

Where is your foundation, faith, focus, fitness, and follow-through? Is it centered on your problems or fixed on the greater things that God has in store for you? Don't ignore your problems, simply *focus* beyond them. When things get bad and obstacles seem like mountains, just *follow through*. Instead of being tossed and turned by worldly affairs, plant your *foundation* in Jesus and the things above. Know that whatever the world has to offer is only temporary and that your *faith* in Christ will break through to the other side. If your mind is set on "things above (Colossians 3:1-3)[79]", then your life will be easier and you won't get so sidetracked. Read Psalm 121:1-2[80] and Isaiah 51:6[81] and always remember that the power to succeed comes from *fitness* in the Lord.

---

[79] Colossians 3:1-3 – Since, then, you have been raised with Christ, set your hearts on things above, where Christ is seated at the right hand of God. Set your minds on things above, not on earthly things. For you died, and your life is now hidden with Christ in God.

[80] Psalm 121:1-2 – I lift up my eyes to the hills–where does my help come from? My help comes from the LORD, the Maker of heaven and earth.

[81] Isaiah 51:5-7 – Lift up your eyes to the heavens, look at the earth beneath; the heavens will vanish like smoke, the earth will wear out like a garment and its inhabitants die like flies. But my salvation will last forever, my righteousness will never fail.

29. Train for Life

Life Lesson: Training for life is similar to training your body to be physically fit.

The martial arts are about physical, mental, and spiritual conditioning. From the first day of class, students work on adjusting their speech, actions, and especially their attitude, among many other things. Some things are harder to change than others, but there's nothing that individuals can't change if they're motivated and serious about working hard. For many, stretching is a difficult area, not only physically, but also mentally. Nonetheless, we are often called to be flexible in various situations and to stretch ourselves to meet certain goals. I am speaking about both stretching your muscles and stretching your comfort-zone in life.

Often when we stretch, we don't notice our progress and it feels like we're getting nowhere. However, the best thing we can do is just hang in there because progress will come. Physical and mental change takes time and patience, and it can even be painful. As we stretch ourselves in the workplace, our social lives, or anywhere in life, we can also become sore as a result. Don't mind the pain because it's only temporary and it's just an indicator that we're doing something right. In order to achieve the desired results of training, we have to accept some short-term disadvantages to reap the long-term advantage of martial competence.

Training can reap results because God created life to be incredibly adaptable. Just take a look at microevolution and how creatures of all different types have adapted over the years. I believe that God intended us to be in a constant state of modification because all of life is a training camp. We're constantly being trained in our minds, bodies, and spirits. Some say it's too hard to memorize information, learn new things, become physically fit, achieve certain goals, get close to God, and live a righteous life; I say that it's all a matter of training. Sure, it may be tough, but it can be done with the right approach. Professional athletes don't start out with the ability to do incredible things. They set up a schedule, train one step at a time, and most importantly, persevere.

"Everyone who competes in the games goes into strict training. They do it to get a crown that will not last; but we do it to get a crown that will last forever" (1 Corinthians 9:25). God will never ask you to do something impossible. If He asks you to do something, then He always provides a way. He's the ultimate coach as you train in every area of life. Like physical and mental training take exercise, spiritual training takes daily Bible reading, regular Bible study, frequent worship, and surrounding yourself in a variety of ways with the positive spiritual influences of your brothers and sisters in Christ. With God's strength, wisdom, and because of the work He did for you on the cross, you can compete and win. The prize (the crown that lasts forever) can be had by all!

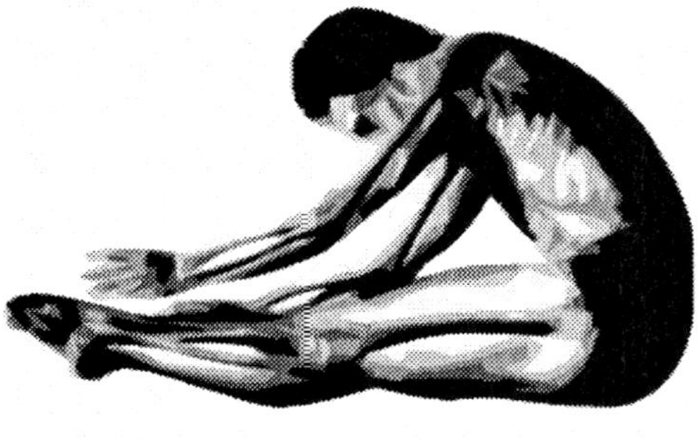

30. Lessons from the Geese

Life Lesson: Teamwork is easier on individuals and benefits many.

Lessons from the Geese is a story that has been around since at least 1972 and shared by many authors in several different works. Dr. Robert McNeish, a biologist who penned this analogy of the geese and their collaborative instincts, knew the advantages of teamwork and applied it to all aspects of life.

Lesson 1: As each bird flaps its wings, it creates an "uplift" for the birds behind it. By flying in a V formation, the whole flock adds a flying range that is significantly better than each bird flying alone. McNeish's lesson is that people who share common direction and a sense of community can get where they are going quicker and easier because they are traveling on the thrust of one another. Many martial artists think of their training as an individual effort; however, I maintain that training is very much a team sport. Students don't only learn from their instructors, they learn from all their fellow classmates, too. By watching carefully, we can also learn from other people's mistakes and successes in all aspects of our everyday lives.

Clearing a path through the jungle of our journey can be very taxing. We need the support and wisdom of others. Look at those who have gone before you and learn from their successes and failures. Children, reap the harvest of wisdom from your parents. Workers, be mindful of all the knowledge your predecessors and supervisors have to offer. Everyone, heed the words of the elders, for their wisdom and experience in life can be a blessing. These people are the leading geese and their uplift can help us rise to the top more quickly. If you can help people in some way, then you should take the lead also by supporting and creating an uplift for others to fly.

Even the great Moses needed support from others on his team (Exodus 17:12[82]).

Lesson 2: When the leading goose gets tired, it rotates back into the formation and another goose flies at the point. McNeish's lesson is that it pays to share leadership and take turns. Throughout my years of experience in both the martial arts and the church, I've found that independent leadership isn't very successful. If we either insist on, or are forced to go it alone, we miss all the benefits that others have to offer. New perspectives, fresh ideas, and blasts of enthusiasm can add wonders to any program. The burden of leadership also becomes too heavy over time, No matter how much energy a person may have to begin with, everyone gets tired (mentally and physically) after a while. When others are there to take the reins from time to time, the leader has a chance to get the much-needed rest that he or she desires. If you happen to be in a situation where you're always flying in the lead position, my encouragement is to occasionally drop back in formation and allow someone else to take point. Swoop down and land on a deserted island for a rejuvenating vacation.

Lesson 3: The geese in formation honk from behind to encourage those in front to keep up their speed. McNeish's lesson is that we need to make sure our honking from behind is encouraging, not discouraging. In churches, in homes, in schools, and in my martial arts organization, I've witnessed situations where attackers have thrown words at their victims with such intensity that the piercing wounds to the heart were only slightly less traumatic than if the assailant had used an actual knife. On the contrary, I've seen encouraging words empower, motivate, and even reduce the presence of old scars left behind from the discouraging words of others. Make no

[82] Exodus 17:12 – When Moses' hands grew tired, they took a stone and put it under Him and he sat on it. Aaron and Hur held his hands up–one on one side, one on the other–so that his hands remained steady till sunset.

mistake; words are powerful! In Ephesians 4:29[83], we are encouraged to build each other up with our words. Used correctly, our words can be a blessing to others and build up those around us. However, if we're not careful, our words can damage others beyond imagination. Therefore, the next time you think about honking, stop and think about the noise you're making and the impact it has on others.

Lesson 4: When a goose gets sick, wounded, or shot down, two other geese drop out of formation and follow it down to help and protect it. They stay with it until it is either able to fly again or dies. Then, they launch out on their own, with another formation or catch up with the flock. McNeish's lesson is that if we have as much sense as the geese, we'll stand by each other just as they do. One thing is for sure, none of us can stay flying high all the time. Whether we're shot down, get sick, or simply become exhausted and can't fly anymore, eventually we all become grounded. Second to worshiping Him, God created every one of us to fulfill a role in His community.

Therefore, as He states in the first half of Genesis 2:18[84], we were not meant to be alone. We need each other. We need the companionship, the love, the support, and sometimes simply just the presence of others in our lives. I am especially saddened when I see the abuse and neglect of the elderly in the world. Too often, these wonderful members of our community are pushed aside by the fast pace and selfishness of our society. Unfortunately, the physically and mentally challenged, the immobile or shut-ins, the depressed, and many of those who just aren't like us are also sometimes

---

[83] Ephesians 4:29 – Do not let any unwholesome talk come out of your mouths, but only what is helpful for building others up according to their needs, that it may benefit those who listen.

[84] Genesis 2:18 – The LORD God said, "It is not good for the man to be alone."

victims of our neglect. We are to love all those who are God's children. We are to participate in fellowship with even those who might be outside of our social circles. We are to reach out to others by lending a hand and giving our support. As with the geese, let us not forget about our fellow brothers and sisters in need and see them through until they can fly again.

31. Recognize Your Limits

Life Lesson: In order to help to others, we must maintain our own health and safety (mentally, physically, and spiritually).

When approaching a situation where someone else is in danger, I tell my students to always assess. Take time to evaluate where and how you might be able to do the most good. For example, if there are many attackers, or if there are weapons involved, and jumping in to help would be placing you in unreasonable danger, then you should probably just go get help. Let's say you're approaching a convenience store and see a person inside being held at gunpoint. Do you go inside and risk getting yourself (and others) injured, or do you get to a phone and ensure that the police are alerted? If you are injured, then you aren't fit to do much of anything for other people.

You must first take care of your own basic needs in order to help with the needs of others. I was reminded of this principle while I was recently being re-certified for CPR. The instructor taught us to always assess situations and take care of our own needs ahead of others. She used an example that we shouldn't approach someone that has been electrocuted by a power line. If you have flown in an airplane, then you are aware that parents are always instructed to put on their own oxygen masks before trying to help their children, in the case of an emergency. Not only are you useless if you don't take care of yourself, but you are often a burden for others.

This principle doesn't only apply to our physical lives, but to our mental and spiritual lives as well. If parents don't assess their needs and take time to be healthy, how can they effectively help their children? Parents who neglect themselves and/or their relationship with each other soon find that the quality of care that they're giving their children is less than adequate. Every parent should take a little time alone with his or her spouse and take vacations. Vacations don't necessarily have to be the big elaborate expensive kind; anything to "get away" will do. Consider all aspects of your mental, spiritual, and physical health for the ultimate good of others. If not, you may become sick (less effective) or merely incapable of helping them.

Now wait just a minute, aren't we supposed to put others ahead of ourselves? Aren't we supposed to watch out for selfishness and not feed our self-interests? As in all things, we need to find balance. I'm not encouraging you to put your own needs first by cutting ahead of others or taking the last piece of pizza. I'm talking about maintaining your mental, spiritual, and physical health by meeting your basic, critical needs. I'm talking about guarding your safety and avoiding complete exhaustion or even a breakdown.

God recognizes the need for taking time out, so why shouldn't we? In His wisdom, He created the holy Sabbath, the seventh day of creation when He took time to rest. God then gave us this day to restore our mental, physical, and spiritual energy. Read Mark 1:35[85]. Here we see that even Jesus needed to take time to get away to a solitary place for a while. The Bible only states that He prayed; however, I speculate that His continuous work was taking a toll on His mind and body and He also needed to recover. Afterwards, He was again ready to travel, preach, and drive out demons throughout Galilee.

As long as we are ultimately meeting our own needs for the purpose of better helping and serving others, and fulfilling God's intent for our lives, then we have no reason to worry. We should not feel guilty about taking time out. When we understand that helping ourselves means we are equipped to help others, we can feel a lot better, accomplish so much more, and create a better community for everyone.

---

[85] Mark 1:35 – Very early in the morning, while it was still dark, Jesus got up, left the house and went off to a solitary place, where He prayed.

32. Take Initiative

Life Lesson: Taking initiative is being a follower of and a leader in Christ.

Throughout my life, I've been involved in a wide variety of groups and organizations. Although these groups and organizations are all very different from each other, they share something in common, not one of them is perfect. I've learned that even though I may think the grass is greener somewhere else, I'll never find a lawn that doesn't have at least a weed or two here and there. The way I see it, I can take different approaches when tackling this disillusion. I can keep quiet and accept the imperfection(s). I can walk away and disassociate myself from that group altogether. While there may be some situations where these options could be appropriate, keeping quiet about defects or quitting generally aren't productive.

Unfortunately, our society has grown to accept, and even encourage the selfish way out. I've seen quite a lot of people (including me) that have discarded their relationships or abandoned their communities because of conflict or dissatisfaction. Where has our commitment gone? What happened to dedication and loyalty? Divorce rates are on the rise, civic organizations are declining in membership, and voter turnout for the elections is diminishing. People just don't want to get involved and commit the time and energy it takes to make a difference. Especially in the martial arts, I've noticed a considerable number of folks who switch schools or drop out all together because of trivialities. I chalk it up to our disposable society.

In addition to the indifference that prevails in our society, I've also noticed that we've become accustomed to avoiding personal conflict with each other. Some people just don't realize that disagreements are part of life and that it's alright for things to get rough sometimes (not physically). On the other hand, it's not alright for things to always run smoothly. You see, conflict has a purpose; it makes our relationships stronger. A great way to test the strength of your relationships is to watch behaviors in the midst of and after conflict. Is the response "I'm outta here" or is it solution-oriented? Has the electronic age made it so convenient to communicate impersonally (text messaging, email, etc.), that we've forgotten how to communicate interpersonally? Have technological advancements made it too easy to be alone?

When faced with a situation that is less than optimal, we should resolve to do something about it. I've spent a lot of time encouraging my students to stand up and take charge of certain aspects of the karate school. One small example is the institution of a social-activities committee. After hearing that students wanted to have more fellowship outside of the karate class, I encouraged some of them to step up and take charge. After all, people don't have a right to complain about unless they have first taken steps to resolve or better the situation.

Of course, we can't just take charge without proper authority and authorization. It's important to recognize and understand the boundaries in which we live and operate and work within them. Just because I may see a need for a speed bump in the trailer park I live in, doesn't give me the right to start pouring concrete. However, it would be appropriate for me to approach the park owner and maybe even the town council with my idea or a more detailed plan. Maybe then I could *help* with fundraising for the project.

Another area in which I encourage my students to take initiative is in relating to others. I strongly encourage them to seek help from others when practicing their techniques. They learn quickly that people who make the initial move are more likely to be successful than those who don't. Sometimes there's a little apprehension involved in approaching people and putting that first foot forward. However, most people are extremely nice and generous with their time if they are only asked. I have found this to be true in almost any setting. If I break the ice, 99% of all the strangers I talk to are happy to speak with me and are themselves enthusiastic about being friendly. Most of the time, when people aren't talking to you, it's because they think that you don't want to talk to them. Take the initiative and strike up a conversation. Make the effort to develop a relationship. Although you may not know it yet, the world is full of folks who are eager to befriend you.

From a Christian perspective, there's an incredible need among non-believers. God is not satisfied with His kingdom yet and is calling us to take initiative in making it bigger and better. Unfortunately, there are people who we know and love, which will not be joining us in Heaven because nobody has taken the initiative to help them establish a relationship with God. As much as a fluffy fairytale that some people make the afterlife out to be, Hell is a very real place. Judgment day is coming, and those who don't have faith in Christ will be very surprised at the outcome! We need to evangelize and be active in building up followers of Jesus.

So, do God's will by sharing the Good News. Too often, we wait around and assume that sharing hope, which can only be found in Jesus, is someone else's responsibility. Even I have far too often waited around for other people to do *my* work. Think twice before saying, "My relationship with God is my own business, and it doesn't involve anyone else." The Great Commission commands something very different (Matthew 28:19)[86], to share our faith with others as we go about our business in the world. Our faith is not a private, personal matter. The Lord wants us to make our faith public, and that means stepping out of our comfort zones and talking with folks about Jesus and all He offers. This is the ultimate initiative that we must take.

---

[86] Matthew 28:19 – Therefore go and make disciples of all nations, baptizing them in the name of the Father and of the Son and of the Holy Spirit.

33. Cognitive Dissonance

Life Lesson: The ego doesn't accommodate dissonance; it kicks it out even at the expense of what's good and right.

The year was 1988, and I was on my way to talk to the landlord who held the lease for my karate school. Things were a little tight in the tuition department back then, so I was going to ask for an extension on my rent. I had the whole conversation all worked out in my mind and knew exactly how I'd ask the landlord when the subject came up. He met me at the front door and we immediately started conversing. In the beginning of our conversation, he asked me about my previous training and experience, and I told him that I was well trained and quite proficient in the martial arts. As he continued to question me, I proceeded to tell him all about the success I had growing up in martial arts. It wasn't long before I had painted an impressive picture of myself and was feeling quite good about my success.

Then he dropped the big bomb on me. "Do you really think you'll be able to make it teaching martial arts?" he asked. In hindsight, I now realize that this was more like a motivational challenge than an innocent question. He threw out the bait and I chomped on it like a hungry fish at dusk, feeding on a pond full of mosquitoes. "Of course I can make it," my ego replied. It was at this point that I knew he had me. How could I possibly ask him for an extension on the rent now? To do so would be to admit that I wasn't doing as well as I had expressed. So what did I do? I wrote the man a check and proceeded to shuffle money, put things on my credit card, and borrow what I could to make it through the rest of the month. I did everything to cover up my defeat. Today, I give that man a lot of credit; he knew exactly what he was doing.

Not too much later, I was in the market for a car. I had wanted a new one for a while, but I wasn't in a hurry. Mom was kind enough to allow me to drive her car until I could get one of my own. Then, I found a bargain, and my commitment to not making any spur of the moment decisions went out the window. I even tried to wait until the weekend so that I could approach my decision with a clear mind, but that didn't work either. In fact, I didn't even make it out of the building before signing on the dotted line. My ego got the best of me and I was played for a fool on that day, too. The car salesperson used a different strategy than my landlord used. He had me thinking that I deserved the vehicle, that I was independent enough to buy it on my own (I was barely 18 at the time), and that I was successful enough to afford it.

I can still hear the words he used to close the deal. "If you don't think you can come up with the money, maybe you shouldn't buy it," he stated. Again, I recognize my error in hindsight. Yet once again, my ego gave way and bowed down to the superior tactics of a master of words. I wasn't about to admit to him (and to myself) that I couldn't handle the payments. He had done such a good job of getting me to reveal so much about myself that I was really thinking that he must like me and be interested in me as a person. Something inside of me took over and I wasn't about to allow him change his mind. Consequently, I began to shift even more money around at the karate school, take out more loans, and apply for more credit cards in order to deal with my financial struggles. Ouch!

In 1957, a social psychologist by the name of Leon Festinger came up with the well-known *Theory of Cognitive Dissonance*[87]. Dissonance occurs when we are faced with inconsistency between our beliefs and behaviors. Since dissonance produces tension and stress, the theory is that we try to eliminate it by either reducing the significance of the beliefs or actions, removing the beliefs or actions altogether, or acquiring new beliefs or actions.

---

[87] Festinger, Leon. Theory of Cognitive Dissonance. Stanford: Stanford UP, 1957.

In both stories at the beginning of this chapter, other people (consciously or unconsciously) used dissonance to get me to behave in the way that they wanted me to behave. Because of my ego, I made some adjustments so that my beliefs and actions would be consistent. With the landlord, I adjusted my actions, and with the car salesman, I adjusted my beliefs. The car salesman told me that he had purchased the same car for his daughter and convinced me with his firsthand experience that it was great. So, after I bought the car, I convinced myself that mom's old car wouldn't have lasted much longer anyway and that the new car was cheaper and safer for me to be driving. I wasn't about to let myself believe that I had made a rash decision.

What sort of things motivate you to change your beliefs or your actions? Do you, as I often do, develop a positive attitude towards something because you feel a need to justify why you're doing it? Are you being manipulated by others into doing things that you might not normally choose to do under different circumstances? Are you manipulating others by using this theory of cognitive dissonance?

Consider an Aesop[88] fable, *The Fox and the Grapes*[89]. One day, there was a famished fox who was trying to get some grapes that were hanging from a vine that was very high and out of reach. She tried everything she could, but just couldn't get them. After quite some time had passed, and the fox was extremely tired, she finally gave up and hid her disappointment by saying, "The grapes are sour, and not as sweet as I had thought." It's easy to justify or make excuses for what we can't seem to accomplish in life. Nonetheless, we all need to learn to recognize when we're fooling ourselves into believing what we know is not true, just to save our egos.

---

[88] Aesop was a slave in Ancient Greece in the mid-sixth century BC. He was only known for his fables, which are still used today in the form of moral lessons and subjects for various types of entertainment.
[89] Æsop. (Sixth century B.C.) Fables. The Harvard Classics. 1909–14.

Admittedly, there are many obstacles in the martial arts that can seem like grapes hanging just beyond our reach. It can be very discouraging, but before you give up so easily, know that some things in life are supposed to be difficult. Those people who have determination eventually find a way to succeed. Unfortunately, there are also people (like the fox) who forego determination to whine, complain, and embellish themselves in disappointment when the grapes don't seem attainable. I'd like to be able to say that most people can accept their disappointment, learn from it, and move on in a mature and responsible fashion; however, it wouldn't be true. There's always someone else to blame! It's easier to say things like "the grapes are sour, and not as sweet as I had thought," than to continue trying to reach them.

Therefore, let us all use caution when lashing out at others and making excuses when things don't go our way. In the dojo, understand that it's okay not to meet a particular goal. It doesn't mean you should give up or change your beliefs about the goal. Pick yourself up, form a strategic plan as to what you can do differently next time, and go after your goal again. If there happens to be a legitimate claim against another who is responsible for your disappointment, follow responsible conflict resolution techniques. Walking away and making excuses (as the fox did) won't do anybody any good. Sure, you'll feel better by convincing yourself that the grapes were sour, but in the long term, you'll wish you had faced the fact that they were really sweet.

Aesop and Festinger may have called our attention to this syndrome in recent years, but I assure you that it's been around for as long as man and woman have walked the Earth. Read Romans 7:14-20[90]. There are many things that we know

---

[90] Romans 7:14-20 – We know that the law is spiritual; but I am unspiritual, sold as a slave to sin. I do not understand what I do. For what I want to do I do not do, but what I hate I do. And if I do what I do not want to do, I agree that the law is good. As it is, it is no longer I myself who do it, but it is sin living in me. I know that nothing good lives in me,

to be right and correct, but do we do them? Or do we do the opposite? We know in our hearts what is right, but we often end up following sinful ways instead. Unfortunately, our society's way of dealing with this dissonance is to change our beliefs about sin and evil. Abortions are justifiable, homosexual behavior is reasoned away, and we fool ourselves into thinking that we actually deserve the sin in which we embellish. It's easier to change our beliefs about sin than to admit we fall short and confess that our behavior isn't what it should be. Many people even resort to blaming others for their inadequacies just so that they won't have to admit to themselves that they're actually responsible for their own actions and decisions.

If only people would realize that God is already aware of our shortcomings, then they wouldn't have to hide. We wouldn't have to pretend anymore. He's waiting for us, ready to offer us His grace and forgiveness for what we've done. Being a Christian isn't about having to be a perfect person, it's about realizing and admitting our faults and looking to Christ for forgiveness and salvation. What a relief! We don't have to carry that heavy load anymore. We don't have to live with the façade of self-sufficiency. Because of Jesus Christ, we no longer have to wrestle with the dissonance in our lives that wrenches at the very unity of our soul. Unity between our beliefs and behaviors has been achieved.

---

that is, in my sinful nature. For I have the desire to do what is good, but I cannot carry it out. For what I do is not the good I want to do; no, the evil I do not want to do–this I keep on doing. Now if I do what I do not want to do, it is no longer I who do it, but it is sin living in me that does it. So I find this law at work: When I want to do good, evil is right there with me. For in my inner being I delight in God's law; but I see another law at work in the members of my body, waging war against the law of my mind and making me a prisoner of the law of sin at work within my members. What a wretched man I am! Who will rescue me from this body of death? Thanks be to God–through Jesus Christ our Lord!

34. Talent vs. Skill

Life Lesson: Time and hard work is the cocoon that transforms the end of talent into the beginning of skill, and the egg that hatches skill from scratch.

Over the years that I've spent teaching martial arts, I've come to understand that there are differences between the talented and the skilled. Not everybody has talent, but everybody can acquire skill. Some people have talent and develop skill, but strangely enough, many students with talent drop out of the martial arts quicker and more frequently than those that only have skill. This could be because they rely on their talent and don't want to take the time to develop their skill. Or, it could be that having talent isn't challenging like developing skill. While there are some exceptions, the majority of people who develop skill over time, tend to be around the longest.

Talent comes naturally, but skill comes from hard work. Talented people develop skills, but skilful people don't develop talent. For those of us who are not naturally talented, skill is developed with a lot of time, effort, and energy. Looking back on my own life, I realize that I now do best what used to be very difficult. You see, I never possessed any natural talent. In fact, when I started karate lessons as a kid, I was so discouraged with my inability to do even a simple forward roll that I would cry myself to sleep at night. Since then, my tumbling skills have grown to include back rolls, handsprings, flips, and even aerials.

I'm also an extremely flexible person and most people who know me now would assume that my flexibility came easily, when in fact, it was only after years of painful and grueling effort that I was finally able to do a split. Today, stretching is my forte. Not only can I do full splits, both sideways and straddling, but I'm at the point where I can have bricks smashed over my thighs–while I'm suspended in a split between two chairs–from the full force of a swinging sledge hammer. I mention this not to brag, but to prove that it is indeed possible to go from being the worst to the best at anything you are willing to put forth effort. Many skillful people started with absolutely no talent for what they do.

Adversity often breeds commitment. While it's true that it is within some people's character to simply give up when faced with adversity, it is within the character of others to buckle down and work through the problem. Adversity is a crucial crossroads because it's here where a person often decides whether to give up and walk away or to kick in the extra effort that it takes to develop a skill. If a person decides to press on, then it will create a stronger investment and a deeper commitment than before. Commitment fosters hard work and in return, hard work strengthens commitment. This comes from a person's choice to develop their skill. Yes, a choice! Far too many people allow outside conditions to influence their inner choices when they should allow their inner choices to influence their outside conditions.

When I first applied to Concordia University, I wasn't very confident in my ability to do well academically and I certainly wasn't hopeful that they would accept me. You see, I had spent so much time focusing on karate while I was growing up that my school transcripts were among the worst in my class. Having barely passed high school and having been turned down to attend college, I sought a career teaching karate after I graduated. Naturally, I was embarrassed when Concordia University asked to see my high school transcripts. I thought for sure that my goal of attending college would be all over. However, they didn't seem to mind, and I was accepted. Maybe it was the fact that fifteen years had passed since high school and they figured I was ready to be serious about my schoolwork.

In the beginning, I did alright surfing on my talent. My memorization and knack for quick thinking helped me breeze through the tests and acquire an easy 'A' in my first couple of semesters. It was around the beginning of my fourth semester when my talent started running out. That's when things got tough. I was used to sitting in Greek class and masquerading as someone who was smart. I enjoyed looking smart, but I guess I wasn't really learning as well as I could have been. Greek didn't mean much to me, because up until then, it wasn't difficult. Contrary to before, I suddenly had to learn how to make mistakes and become comfortable with my ignorance in front of others. I struggled because I didn't want to look like the fool. I liked others to think that I knew what I was doing and that I was strong and not weak. School was easy when I was relying on talent, but when I started working on developing my skill, I found myself exposed and didn't like it one bit. Somehow, I found the courage to persevere.

Although I thought that I was revealing to the class and my professor that I was unskilled and vulnerable, they already knew it. The professor knew it because he had seen it many times before, and my classmates knew it because they were in the same boat as I. You see, others may have seen me as weak and unconsciously unskilled, but it never bothered me until I saw myself as weak and unskilled. Therefore, how I feel about how others perceive me is all contained within my own self-image. It's through working on these difficult points in life that help us to grab hold of our weaknesses and make them into our strengths. If we can pick up and develop skill even when our talent drops off, then we take ownership in the accomplishment and don't want to part with it. Soon, before we know it, the things we once liked the least, become the very things that we now like the most.

If you want something badly enough, but you're just not talented, then you can accomplish your goal with a few steps. First, admit your weakness in a particular area so you can develop skill. Second, don't impede the learning process as you develop your skill. Set aside your ego and don't be afraid to expose yourself as someone who isn't perfect. I suspect that this was the source of my tears when I was learning front rolls as a young child. My self-esteem was based on what I thought others thought of me. Therefore, I always felt it necessary to put on a front in order to have people like me. Even though it won't always kill the learning process, it sure does slow it down. Third, celebrate your victories. Don't be afraid to give yourself a pat on the back for accomplishing both your long-term and your short-term goals. No matter what it is that you choose, remember that you can do it with the right attitude and perseverance. If an inflexible, uncoordinated, uneducated person like me can make a success out of his weaknesses, I know that you can, too. You can do everything through Him who gives you strength (Philippians 4:13).

35. Dealing with Bullies

Life Lesson: Our first defense against a bully should be to understand what drives his or her behavior.

It's sad when the parents of a perspective student ask me if there's anything I can do for their little Johnny because he's being picked on in school. The majority of parents I talk to don't really know how to handle a bully or prevent their child from being picked on. Bullies come in all shapes and sizes, and especially in school, there are many short-term solutions for dealing with them. I tell parents that the first thing they need to do is make the school aware of this abuse so that the school can take appropriate actions, both in disciplining the aggressor and in protecting the receptor. They also need to know that studying the martial arts is a long-term solution and will not help much in the short-term. Finally, I tell parents about the common misconceptions about bullies.

The first common misconception about bullies is that learning how to fight is the best way to defeat them. While there are cases where self-defense skills are necessary to ward off serious attacks, most confrontations can be avoided by other means. Some of the most effective ways of dealing with a bully are through character traits that take a long time to develop. In almost all cases, bullies seek out and pick on those who are lacking in self-confidence and/or those who are isolated from others. More important than learning how to fight, martial arts can help develop self-confidence and social skills that will repel bullies and avoid the bite of an attack. Even if bullies aren't completely repelled, self-confidence and social skills can keep their bite from stinging. Moreover, bullies are less likely to continue biting if there is no sting.

Another thing that self-confidence does is allow people to recognize their own faults and *make fun* of themselves. If someone purposely picks on me about...oh, let's say, my short height; and I can laugh with him by making a comment about all the money I save by being 35 and still able to shop in the kids department. Then I've just turned the tables on the bully. I've placed us both on even ground. Furthermore, if I can do something to win his friendship (like show interest in him or choose a random act of kindness towards him), then that person is much more likely to consider me a friend and stop picking on me. One important note about this: *every case is unique and no one thing will work in every situation.* I don't want to mislead you into thinking that pacifying bullies is as easy as offering them a lollipop.

There are different levels of severity in bullying. Are the attacks just verbal? Are they mildly physical (pushing, pinching, etc)? Or does the bully pose a very dangerous and serious threat? The solutions I've mentioned may work wonders with the first two types of bullies. However, if you can distinguish that someone is putting you in substantial physical danger and real mental harm, then don't hesitate to get the authorities involved. While learning to deal with a small amount of teasing and schoolyard play is all just a part of growing up, nobody should ever have to endure abuse (mental or physical) which can carry serious consequences for the victim.

The second misconception about bullies is that bringing them to martial arts class will only make things worse, like putting a flamethrower in the hands of an arsonist. Not true (that is, in the right kind of karate school). Since the majority of bullies are actually lacking in self-esteem and are seeking social acceptance, building their self-confidence can only help them come to the realization that they have nothing to prove. For a bully, it's not as important to prove to others how tough they are (although showing off to friends is a part of the equation) as it is for them to prove it to themselves. As their confidence increases through martial arts training, their tactic of putting others down in order to boost themselves up will no longer be necessary. The better we understand what is at the heart of almost every bully's behavior, the better we can combat it and actually help.

After winning some major matches at a tournament one Saturday night, my teammates and I went out to celebrate our victory. It was customary for us to wear T-shirts with our karate school logos out to dinner afterwards to signify that we were all united and one big family. I wasn't expecting the celebration to last beyond the meal, but a few of my friends invited me to go out with them to a bar. I learned that one of our karate associates owned this bar and I decided to go check it out and hang with the guys. Little did I know that the bar was located in a rough part of town. From the moment we arrived, my *spidey sense* was activated and the hair on the back of my neck stood straight up on end. I didn't drink and wasn't particularly fond of some of the activity going on in the front room by the bar, so a friend of mine and I decided to make our way to the pool tables in the back room.

My friend decided to step out to get us some cokes. Coincidentally, just when I was all alone in that secluded room, a group of about eight extremely large unruly guys walked in and began to size me up and down. The leader of the pack noticed my karate shirt and decided that he was going to look tough and show off that night. He approached and challenged me with both his body language and the provoking words that came out of his mouth. Wow, I bet the others in the group really must have thought that he was cool to be using such language and picking on a karate dude. He asked me (and I'll leave out the explicatives) if I thought that I was some big tough guy or something. My response was, "Oh this shirt? No man, it's my brother's." I told him that I wasn't in karate and quickly changed the subject to asking his friends if they'd gotten a look at the girls that were dancing in the bar on their way in.

My intentions were twofold. First, I wanted to make myself seem weaker. Challenging a karate dude was one thing, but it took all the steam out of his engine to find out he was only challenging some meek little 'old guy with no intention of fighting back that day. You see fighting me at that point wouldn't have made him look as good in front of his friends. His victory wouldn't have been nearly as sweet. Now if I had allowed my ego to get in the way, I certainly could have puffed out my chest and taken him on. However, what was the point? I certainly wouldn't have been defending myself and I would have been just as guilty as he was for starting the trouble in the first place. Instead, I won the fight before it ever started. I diffused the situation and used my head to escape a confrontation. My self-esteem was securely in place, and I had absolutely nothing to prove that day.

Second, I diverted his attention away from me and found something that we both could have in common. I wasn't particularly interested in the kind of girls who were in the front room. I preferred wholesome girls, but he didn't need to know anything about my preferences or me. By his thinking that we shared a common thread, we were now on the same side. Furthermore, I didn't make my comment about the girls to him only. By making the comment to the entire group, I was assured a better chance of getting a favorable response and diverting the conversation away from me. My plan worked. I announced that I was going to grab a drink, and they never saw me again.

Understanding bullies and their behaviors can help you in a variety of situations. Using your head (mentally) should always be your first line of defense. Keep in mind though that there will be some instances where self-defense will be unavoidable and using psychological tactics on your opponent won't always work. The last thing I want to do is sugarcoat bullying so much that I do you more harm than good. There are folks who are very streetwise and have more of an agenda than just building up their self-esteem. Their intentions (right from the start) are to do you harm no matter what. The key is to be able to recognize potentially dangerous and life threatening situations and respond appropriately.

There is a time for talking, a time for psychological diversions, and although it is only as an absolute last resort... there is also a time to employ physical self-defense.

For an interesting story about using psychology in lieu of a physical defense, read "David at Nob" in 1 Samuel 21[91]. In this story, David pretends to be insane in order to avoid a confrontation. David was an excellent strategist and his stories offer us a wealth of information about dealing with enemies.

[91] 1 Samuel 21:13 – So he pretended to be insane in their presence; and while he was in their hands he acted like a madman, making marks on the doors of the gate and letting saliva run down his beard.

36. Facing Problems

Life Lesson: When you confront a problem, you begin to solve it. When you ignore a problem, you make it grow.

One of my biggest pet peeves is simply being ignored. I can understand if people disagree with me, don't like me, or even don't want to see me. However, I can't stand it when people ignore me. Ignoring someone has to be one of the rudest things you can do. In my karate school, you wouldn't believe the number of people who simply just stop coming to class (sometimes after years of being with me). No "good-bye" or "I'm going to take some time off." They just drop off the face of the Earth without any warning and I never see them again. I guess I would feel differently if running a karate school was like any other business, but it's not. I'm with students several times per week, and many of them are like family to me. We spend time together outside of class and share a personal bond, because of our teacher-student relationship.

Because I share my personal life with these folks, it's all the harder for me to comprehend when a student just breaks contact all of the sudden without any warning. As a method of payment, I used to give a substantial discount to folks who would sign up for an *electronic funds transfer* (EFT) from their checking, savings, or credit card. Sure, I was assured to get my money on time every month, but more importantly, EFT stopped people from passively quitting and forced them to talk to me if they wanted to suspend their membership. I certainly don't have a problem with people leaving my karate school. I understand that folks will quit and move on for a variety of reasons. It is just nice and expected that they would at least say goodbye.

It's easy in this day and age to walk away from problems and avoid confrontation and conflict. Even when there's no real problem, sometimes it's still easier for students to walk away than to explain to me why they no longer want to take karate classes. From my view, this behavior is like an ostrich sticking its head in the sand. While ignoring or hiding from a problem may seem to make it disappear, it does not according to Jean Piaget's[92] *Stage Theory*. Between the age of one and four months, babies begin to develop what Piaget called *object permanence*, the realization that an object exists even while it is hidden from view. Until they develop it fully, they are often fascinated with the peek-a-boo game, because they haven't come to the realization that people and things don't just disappear from the face of the Earth when they are covered. Sadly, when it comes to problems, some people just never learn what most babies learn in their first year of life.

With God, we also bury our heads in the sand (like the ostrich) and hide our heads under the blanket (like the baby), especially after recognizing our shortcomings. It's easier to walk away than to remain in a relationship with Him. We may think that He doesn't want us if we're not perfect, or we may figure that there's no sense in a relationship with Him because we can't keep up our end of it. While it's true that none of us live up to all of what God wants for us in our lives, it is no reason to ignore Him. God accepts us unconditionally, and ignoring Him simply stunts our growth and development as human beings. Then, before we know it, we begin to blame Him for our stunted growth and lack of development.

While it is acceptable for many, it is not helpful to ignore or cover up our problems. Hiding is just an easy way out, a way to avoid uncomfortable confrontations. Uneasiness or contention in a relationship should be brought into the light and discussed. Those people who choose to sacrifice their relationships rather than face the uneasiness or contention that all relationships are bound to experience, are indeed very selfish, shallow, and weak. Problems and difficulties in life don't just go away because we turn our backs on them or cover them up…they fester and bring consequences. In fact,

---

[92] Jean Piaget was a Swiss natural scientist and a developmental psychologist well known for his studies with children.

covering up a problem only facilitates its growth. Like a weed that can quickly spread throughout a nicely kept lawn, friction between people can end up overtaking the relationship.

Consider the following story. A man and his wife are driving in their car to a destination across town. They've been married for twenty-five years and in all that time, the wife has almost never sat behind the wheel when the two of them were in the car together. Finally, the wife breaks the silence and says to her husband, "Why is it that we don't sit so close beside one another in the car like we used to do before we were married?" To that the husband replied, "Who moved?" In this story, the wife is to be commended for speaking up and discussing her feelings with her husband. If she had not taken the time to initiate a conversation and tell him how she truly felt, he might have never realized that the distance between them was an issue. The wife's frustration would have swelled and either burst someday or possibly manifested itself within the guise of some unrelated insignificant matter.

This same principle of learning to face problems is applicable to much more than just a person's relationships. There are numerous situations in our world every single day, which need to be dealt with. While I'm not suggesting that individuals should take on all the problems of the entire world, all by themselves, I do think that each person should at least contribute. Whether our contribution is to take a bite out of crime, alleviate world hunger, help to house the homeless, tackle environmental issues, or provide assistance in another way; success can only be achieved by first getting our heads out of the sand and recognizing the problem. Only then can we then take a proactive approach to step up to the plate and make a difference in the world by confronting the problems that affect us as a society and are between us as individuals.

37. Strength from Weakness

Life Lesson: We can use our weaknesses to create strengths in all areas of life.

I was very young when I started martial arts. In fact, I was the youngest in my class, as most of the other students were adults. The martial arts weren't as popular back then. They didn't become very popular until David Carridine, Chuck Norris, Bruce Lee, the Karate Kid, and the Ninja Turtles came about in the 70s and 80s. Consequently, the classes were a lot smaller and the school couldn't yet justify offering separate youth and adult classes. As you can imagine, my small size presented quite a struggle when it came to practicing with adults. I was constantly getting hurt by bigger and stronger guys. They certainly didn't mean to hurt me as often as they did. It's just that they were much bigger and didn't realize how strong they were and how powerful their blows felt to a young kid. I also found myself ready to quit on several different occasions because the bigger and stronger seemed to be advancing faster in rank.

Although it was extremely difficult to keep up with the big guys, I somehow found the strength to hang in there. I received some of that strength from one of my wise mentors. He told me to take it one day at a time, and to stop comparing myself to others and their ranks. I didn't need to "keep up with the big guys." He taught me to be my own person and focus on my own personal goals. He also taught me to stop focusing on my weaknesses. If we become consumed with all the things that we can't do, or with all the things that others do better than we do, we'd be nothing but depressed. Instead, his advice was to take the things that I did well, and capitalize on them. From that point on, I made it a point to turn my attitude around and begin some serious training. Not only did I get better at what I already did well, but before I knew it, I found myself improving in all areas of the martial arts, even areas that I didn't really like.

Fighting was one such area that I just dreaded. The big guys had so much reach on me that they could easily hit me while I was still out of range of being able to hit them back. My short arms just couldn't make contact. So, I lost and got beat up almost every time. The only thing that I could do to compensate was to begin to use my legs more often. I soon discovered that my legs were about the same length as their arms. Therefore, I began kicking my bigger opponents hard in the ribs every time they lifted their arms and stretched out their hands to punch me in the head. After so much time of using my legs to compensate, I soon found that kicking had become my greatest strength. Unbeknownst to me at the time, my technique, speed, flexibility, and power of my kicks were to be the very things that I would become best known for in the martial arts community. Because I had to learn how to compensate for a weakness (my size) when I was a kid, I now have a hook kick that could knock the head off the shoulders of any formidable opponent.

From that experience, I learned to concentrate on what I can do instead of what I can't. We can use our weaknesses to create strengths in all areas of life. For example, I know a person in ministry who stutters uncontrollably and hence has a very difficult time delivering sermons. Nonetheless, that person has come to be a fantastic writer. I also know of a person who is confined to a wheelchair, but has turned out to be one of the best martial arts teachers ever. Her ability to use her hands and instruct others, in spite of the challenges she faces with her legs, is an inspiration. My mother, in spite of her physical limitations, developed her quilt making skills and created some of the most beautiful quilts that I've ever seen. No matter what it is in your life that you're lacking (and everybody has something), don't be hung up over it. Stop dwelling on the negative by only seeing the *cannots* in life, and start seeing the *cans*. Take what some might consider a weakness and turn it around to create strength.

When it comes to weaknesses, I celebrate everyday that I'm spiritually lacking. What I mean is that if I didn't have any deficiencies, then I wouldn't have a need for Christ. The weaker I am, the stronger He is. His strength lives out in my weakness and imperfections. The fact that I don't measure up makes it all the more apparent that He is perfect and lives up to every standard that I can't. What a tragedy it would be if I were to become so self-sufficient in my own strength that I had no need or want for God. Now I'm not saying that God wants me to be sinful and weak, He doesn't. He would like nothing more than for me to be flawless like Him. However, the reality is that I'm not. We're not. So let's not focus on the negative. Let's focus on the positive and how He turned our weakness around into something good. We can set our sights on the loving perfect God whose sole purpose for taking the form of a man was to ensure that we received His power, strength, and forgiveness in order to have eternal life with Him in Heaven. In His love and power is our strength.

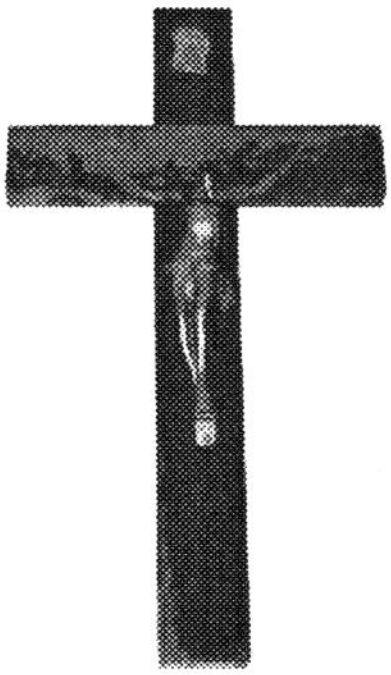

38. Pain is Our Friend

Life Lesson: Pain always directs us, not only physically, but in all areas of life.

Fifty push-ups, one-hundred sit-ups, a half-hour of running on a treadmill...sounds painful, right? Exercising certainly can be, and in fact, should be. Pain is necessary for achieving our goals. When exercising, we need to push ourselves beyond what is easy and comfortable in order to make any note-worthy progress. If every time I did pushups, I stopped after only three or four because that's how many I could do comfortably, then I'd never be able to reach my objective of ten or fifteen. It's the same way with any exercise. We must work hard and push our bodies to their limits in order to make any sort of significant progress. As the saying goes, *no pain, no gain.*

Nonetheless, there are different types of pain. Pain that results from pushing our muscles to the limit is a sign of getting stronger. Somebody once told me that this kind of pain is weakness leaving your body, so in martial arts we try to invoke it. However, the sharp muscle-ripping, ligament-tearing, tear-jerking pain that accompanies a serious injury is something we obviously don't want to invoke. This second type of pain does us a favor by telling our mind when to make our body quit. Have you ever touched a hot stove? It's a good thing that our bodies tell us to stop before we do permanent damage to ourselves. No matter the type, pain is beneficial.

Pain is a wonderful teacher. It establishes boundaries in which we operate. It sets parameters so we know how far to the left or right we can maneuver. Without its warnings, we may inadvertently be injured or killed. Pain teaches us not to repeat specific behaviors, which can be dangerous. Once hurt, we're more likely to remember that we should avoid certain activities. This has physical implications for body mechanics as well as applications for life in general. Pain definitely has much instruction to offer in martial arts training and in keeping physically healthy in general. However, the same lessons that pain has to offer us physically can also help us in our relationships with others, our mental and spiritual health, and our emotional well-being.

Aside from the mind and body, pain is a well-received friend in our spiritual lives. Spiritual pain is never pleasant. However, if we focus on the positive, we can see that pain is valuable in the larger scheme of life. Without pain, humanity would be too self-centered and wouldn't find a need for God. It's the pain and suffering that we've experienced here on earth that has awakened our sense of need and encouraged us to seek Him. Now I'm not saying that God put pain and suffering in the world just so that we'd turn to Him; pain and suffering were brought into the world by our sin. However, God can and does use situations that are negative and turns them around into something positive. He is therefore capable of using pain to move us to repent and turn from evil.

Satan would love nothing more than for us to remain separated from God and suffer in eternity. After all, misery loves company. It's when our souls ache inside that we often find the need for our Lord's comfort. We turn to our Father like a little child crying out to a parent when he's just fallen off his bike and scraped his knee. Assuredly, we find that God is just waiting for us with outstretched arms. He gives us a big bear hug and tells us that everything is going to be alright. The pain might still hurt for a short time; however, we can count on the assurance that there's a better home waiting for us with our Father in Heaven. It's a place filled with peace and joy, where God's love surrounds us, fulfills our every need, and wipes away every pain.

39. The Road Less Traveled

Life Lesson: The secret is in the journey, not the destination.

One of the biggest problems that we face in the martial arts today is that there is so much emphasis on obtaining the *'oh' so coveted* black belt that some students miss out on what it truly means to be in the martial arts. Those that spend their time in want of the physical belt can sorely miss all the beauty and benefits that can be harvested in the journey of accomplishing that dream. Of course getting your black belt is certainly nice, I just don't recommend it being your only focus in the martial arts. If your existence rests solely on the black belt, then what will happen once you achieve it? From what I've seen, you will probably encounter a severe letdown and feel lost without any more direction or motivation as to where to head next. I've seen too many newly promoted black belts that suffer from this syndrome.

The problem is that there is so much emphasis placed on the black belt being the ultimate goal that students feel as if they've finished once they've arrived. Indeed, nothing could be further from the truth. If anything, the rank of black belt is only the beginning. It is where the fundamentals of martial arts become a strong enough foundation for the real training to take place. In order for the learning process to continue, a student must lose herself in this training, and not in her rank. It's like competing in a tournament. Sure, there is some pleasure in winning a trophy; however, the real joy comes in the thrill of competition and the strides gained in becoming a better martial artist. It's not the trophy that is the goal; it's the process by which one wins it. A great student realizes that achieving black-belt status is not a destination, but a journey without an end.

Unfortunately, many people miss life because they focus too much on the destination and not enough on the journey. How many people bust their chops to achieve what they consider the American Dream, meanwhile everything and everyone that they encounter along the way quietly slips by without being noticed? How many people spend 30 to 40 years in a job they don't really like, with their only real goal being retirement? These people fail to realize the beauty of daily process and miss all the pleasure that the journey of life has to offer. We are not a destination, we are a journey. If we were a destination, then our birth would be our arrival, and there would be no growth, development, or change. For some reason, God designed life to be a journey. He brought you and me into this world as babies and we've been traveling on our own unique and incredible journey ever since. In the end, there are really only two destinations: Heaven and Hell.

Life is meant to be a journey, not a destination. It's not about arriving at a certain point in our spirituality or obtaining some sort of tangible religious goal. While going to Heaven should be a goal for all of us to obtain, it shouldn't be our only focus. Our entire Christian life should be focused on our journey with God. Life is about our faith in Christ and the growing relationship with our Lord that it brings. So, let's enjoy the wonderful blessings and joy that comes from being in communion with our Lord right now, today. John Ruskin once said, "The highest reward for man's toil is not what he gets for it, but what he becomes by it." Unlike a tournament, we get no awards for first place in our spiritual lives. Instead, our lives are enriched through experience.

40. Strive for Excellence

Life Lesson: If you aim towards perfection, you can only fall short at excellence.

I tell my students to strive for excellence and aim towards perfection, even though they know that perfection is unattainable. I want them to accept the reality that they'll never be perfect. Because none of us is or ever will be perfect, we must learn to live with our imperfections, and the imperfections of others. We *aim towards perfection* because we need 100% of our effort to get us as close as possible. If we do our very best in attempting to reach flawlessness, then we *fall short at excellence.* It doesn't matter how close we come to reaching perfection. Pass or fail; win or lose; anyone who puts forth an outstanding effort has indeed achieved excellence. Therefore, even though I expect a lot from my students, I am also very understanding and forgiving when it comes to making mistakes and not being perfect.

Patience and understanding are qualities, which are vital for good instructors. Students know that doing their best is all we ever expect. After all, training to get better is the reason why we train in the first place. If we all had perfect students, then our job as instructors would be obsolete. If a student had to be perfect in order to join the school, there would, in fact, be no reason for him to join. Now that's job security! For as long as there are imperfect people in the world, there will always be a need for teachers. Keep in mind, though, that teachers are just students themselves that are slightly further ahead on the path of learning. Teachers are also far from perfect. In short, we all have plenty to keep us busy at gaining enough wisdom and self-improvement to last us a lifetime.

As a student needs a karate school to learn, Christians need Christ because they're not perfect. Any Christians who try to tell you that they're perfect are not Christians at all. If you are perfect, you don't need Jesus; and if you don't need Jesus, you're not a Christian. Consequently, church is full of sinners, and even those who don't practice what they preach can have our Lord's forgiveness and will enjoy eternal life with God in Heaven. Thank you, Lord, for knowing that we would be imperfect, loving us anyway, and executing a plan to rescue us (Jesus' death on the cross). All of this in spite of our failures! Now I can rejoice and rest easy knowing that through my faith in Him I can claim victory and achieve true excellence in my life. I can live my life to be the best I can be in response to the grace and mercy I have already received from Christ.

Because we are children of God, we can be free to live life to its fullest and get the most out of what it has to offer. We can rejoice in our walk with the Lord, grow as human beings, and share our God-given gifts with those around us who may need a helping hand. Therefore, let's aim towards perfection in all aspects of our lives and use the ideals in the Bible and in this book. I pray that none of us will become complacent with who we are and stop trying to better ourselves. No matter who we are, there will always be room for growth. So join me on my journey as I endeavor to work on these things for my own life. Writing this book was as helpful for me as I hope reading it has been for you.

Miscellaneous Information

USA Martial Arts: www.UsaMartialArts.net
~For more information about Master Brown or his system of Issho-Ryu Karate

The Christian Martial Arts Network: www.agapy.com/cma
~For more information about Christ-centered martial arts and an updated directory of associations and schools

---

Other books by Agapy Publishing:

Christian Martial Arts 101 (2004)
ISBN *Regular Edition:* 0972132813
ISBN *Instructor Edition:* 0972132821

Christian Martial Arts 101 explains the major principles of Christian martial arts and includes 101 Bible lessons for use in the classroom and at home. This book features an awesome, powerful ministry that prepares and equips youths for all aspects of Christian life and service.

Martial Arts: The Christian Way (2002)
ISBN: 0972132805

"In *Martial Arts–The Christian Way*, Wendy Williamson presents an exciting concept that strengthens children's bodies, minds, and souls and helps us to raise capable, disciplined, Christian leaders. If you are a parent, minister, or teacher, this book should be your constant reference."

~Joseph Lumpkin, President of Karate for Christ

Printed in the United States
56821LVS00002B/304-426

9 780972 132855